3⁰⁰

TOWARD THE SUMMIT

TOWARD
THE SUMMIT

By

Raymond Leopold Bruckberger

DOMINICAN

Translated by

SISTER M. CAMILLE, O.S.F.
AND ALASTAIR GUINAN

P. J. KENEDY & SONS

NEW YORK

TOWARD THE SUMMIT

is a translation of three French works by Father Bruckberger: *Credo in Unum Deum* (*Revue Thomiste,* Desclée de Brouwer) ; *Rejoindre Dieu* (Paris, Gallimard); *La Valeur Humaine du Saint* (Cahiers du Rhône).

Cum Permissu Superiorum

Nihil Obstat: JOHN A. GOODWINE, S.T.L., J.C.D.
Censor Librorum

Imprimatur: ✠ FRANCIS CARDINAL SPELLMAN
Archbishop

New York, July 20, 1956

The Scripture translations throughout are in the translation of Monsignor Ronald Knox; OLD TESTAMENT, Volume I, copyright 1948, Sheed and Ward, Inc., New York; OLD TESTAMENT, Volume II, copyright 1950, Sheed and Ward, Inc., New York; NEW TESTAMENT, copyright 1944, Sheed and Ward, Inc., New York. Used with permission.

To

*The Contemplative Cloistered Dominican Sisters
of Rosary Shrine, Summit, N.J.*

CONTENTS

I

CREDO IN UNUM DEUM

Translated by
Sister M. Camille, O.S.F.

CREDO IN UNUM DEUM

W<small>HY IS IT SO</small> <small>DIFFICULT</small> to speak to men about God?

If I should return from Russia after having been received by Bulganin, and having had a long and cordial conversation with him, I would suddenly find myself in the limelight. Journalists would rush to interview me and publish my photograph. All my friends would remember me and invite me to dinner so that I might tell them all about it.

That I may know God is of no particular interest to anyone. People do not like to hear about Him. Things often take place as if God were the secret and positive enemy of man. It is no longer even a question of the unknown God, to whom the Athenians raised altars. We do not wish to hear about God any more. It is as if we already knew Him too well, as if He were formerly numbered among our most intimate friends, and had since insulted us and betrayed us so often that it is henceforth forbidden to speak of Him in our presence or even to name Him. God is taboo. We are not at variance with Him, it is even worse; for us it is the same as if He were dead. Nietzsche saw clearly that such is the Annunciation of the modern world: G<small>OD IS</small> <small>DEAD</small>.

To anyone who would seek to be assured of a warm welcome in such company it might well be recommended: "Above all, not a word about God or anything concerning Him! Do not even say that you know Him! The door would be closed in your face!"

One must take things and people as they are, at least when one aspires not to be obeyed, but primarily to be understood. It is more difficult to reconcile old friends who have become mortal enemies than to bring together amicably persons who do not know one another at all. God is not exactly unknown to us; that is what is grave. In the innermost depths of our being we will have nothing of Him. When one speaks to men about God one almost always encounters a secret desire either that He may not exist, or that we may have nothing to do with Him.

There is something more besides. Even when one comes to the point of speaking about God to those who have the faith and who admit religion as a whole, one encounters another secret desire: that God may be in their resemblance and in the image which they themselves make of Him. They readily quote Pascal and his: "God perceptible to the heart." God completely fills the heart of man, but it must be understood that He will not overflow its limits and, above all, that He will not break it. To be sure, this heart must be pure. But pride, too, has its purity. There is a temptation to stoicism at the inmost core of Christianity. This type of Christian easily affects scorn of the intelligence, and I am not so sure that such Christians are not idolaters.

They fashion for themselves a convenient and portable God, like a portable radio always tuned in on their own personal wave length. God perceptible to the heart? But suppose they make a God of their

heart? They reassure themselves in thinking of all the
sacrifices which this God has already cost them. But
all gods are exacting and costly. Since the beginning
of things, how many sacrifices, and cruel ones, were
offered to them on the mountains? It was not always
to the true God. Men have immolated their own children to idols of bronze or to some Astartes of flesh
and blood.

It is as difficult to teach about the true God to
idolaters as to those who have literally struck God
off their lists. Well, that is the teaching I am going
to attempt, to both groups.

However much one may be emancipated from social conventions, Christ, nonetheless, remains a very
disconcerting personage. One particular day He had
decided to teach a most important and difficult matter of theology. He did not make an appeal to the
local priest familiar with books and sacred traditions.
He did not even appeal to the apostles. On the contrary, He waited until they had gone. At the edge of
the fountain He began a conversation with a woman
of loose morals, the Samaritan woman. Such creatures at least have a simple and direct mind. That is
without doubt what Christ was seeking.

"Believe me, woman . . . the time is coming, nay,
has already come, when true worshippers will worship the Father in spirit and in truth; such men as
these the Father claims for His worshippers. God is
a spirit, and those who worship Him must worship
Him in spirit and in truth."

The Gospel does not tell us what it cost this woman to receive such teaching. It is probable that she changed her life, for there is no middle way. Either man is spirit, even to his very flesh, or he is flesh, even to his very spirit. Here, indeed, is the question and that is why it is so difficult to speak of God to beings of flesh and blood. God is troublesome to them. When He arrives, He acts as Master and Lord, at home, everywhere. He produces the same effect as one of those frightfully importunate guests who, when his arrival is announced, arouses in us a desire to double-lock the door and go off on a trip. We know very well that, fundamentally, acknowledgment of the true God involves changing one's life.

This reticence of modern man with respect to God proves that he has not been rid of Him to any degree. He is like a man who, once having loved, is afraid of being enamored again if he meets the woman who has made him suffer. Pascal puts these words on Christ's lips: "You would not seek Me if you had not found Me." Our old civilizations have known God and loved Him. They do not want to hear of Him any more, so that they may not be obliged to serve Him. They recall that this service is hard. It remains to be seen whether man can dispense with a master and whether the masters he gives himself are not the worst possible ones.

"In spirit and in truth," says Christ. Here indeed is an honorable language, and a more loyal one than "God perceptible to the heart." Even if it is horrible to fall alive into the hands of God, courage of spirit consists in envisaging such a fate forthrightly. It does not depend on us that God exists or does not exist. The ostrich which buries its head in the sand in order not to see that it is surrounded by hunters has never stood for the symbol of intellectual courage.

The faculty of seeing and of discovering is our intelligence, even more adventuresome than our hearts. It is this intelligence which poses embarrassing questions. It is this intelligence which solicits the loyalty of man and poses this question to the recalcitrant:

Does God exist, yes or no?

Were God the enemy of man, it is man's heart rather than his mind that would evade the question; God is also perceptible to the heart. But the question is raised. It is the mind which must accept the challenge. The sensitivity of a blind man naturally denies the light. His intelligence, nevertheless, puts the problem to him.

But after all, can I not dodge the question? When I am told that courage of mind consists in taking account of whether God exists or not, can I not answer that this is perhaps pure intellectual curiosity and, all in all, rather vain? One can very well get along without knowing and frequenting great personages, and it is even a wise policy to do so. However important God may be, what is He to me? Is it not possible to live and die without knowing Him?

I exist and my life is my own. I am what I am and I belong to myself. I have for my own the honor and joy of living. I close my eyes and withdraw within myself. I feel the warm and faithful complicity of my being. To a greater or lesser degree, the wicked Rich Man is each one of us.

Fool! says the Gospel to him, fool believing that you possess what you have, yet even today your soul will be asked of you.

Fool! It is possible for me to be betrayed even to that degree. This complicity with my being can be torn asunder. I am not sure of myself. I can die before finishing this page. Reader, you could die even before reading it to the end.

Each man knows that he will die. If I remind him of it, it is not in the hope of obtaining from him a terrorized assent to religion. The game of fear would rather provoke defiance in noble souls. I do not take death for a menace, I take it for a fact. A universal fact, inevitable, fatal, and one which, beyond the evidence of the senses, poses to man the question of legitimacy over his very being and his own existence. I say *my life, my being, my existence*. Is it certain that this life, this being, this existence, is my domain and belongs to me? There is the question which death places before us!

A man is accustomed to being absolute master in his own house. Then unexpectedly there arrives an officer who serves a warrant, with papers which prove that this man is but a usurper. This house belongs to another. That other will tolerate him, but one day he will have to vacate the place. One day? Perhaps tomorrow, perhaps in a little while. . . .

Fool! You think you possess what you have. Tomorrow your soul will be required of you.

However beautiful his life may be, even however virtuous it is, this man is the bad Rich Man, who believes that he possesses totally all that he has, forever. Fool!

My life is threatened. My being can be seized from one moment to another. I am constantly under the threat of a warrant for arrest. All is delay, all is respite, all is comedy. I am contradicted even in my own being. The axe is at the root of the tree. There is no lasting reprieve, no recourse. Execution can be delayed, not annulled. Prophets die, tyrants die, slaves die, poor and rich die, saints and sinners die. Ten centuries are like ten years, ten days, ten seconds. Everything is absurd, since nothing is adequate. Nothing has a guarantee, and on every side is the warning that all comes to an end. All things are like specters which rise up before the tent of the King saying:

Despair and die!

★ ★ ★

Well, before dying, I shall try to understand.

For, in fact, to confine myself to determining an absurdity amounts to stopping short in the middle of the way. The law and honor of the intelligence consist in resolving the absurdity, not in becoming established in it. How cowardly and detestable is the position of a being who ontologically is not sufficient to himself and yet subjectively satisfies himself, a being who does not sustain himself and yet to whom one clings for support! The philosophy of the absurd is that of the bad Rich Man, according to the measure of his intelligence. More mad, still, than the one in the Gospel. He knows that he does not possess what he has, he knows that his soul will be required of him and he refuses to take that into consideration. And a reckoning will be exacted of him.

It is said of something absurd that it does not stand up. I grant that man and the world may be absurd and that they do not stand alone, but then who supports them? However unsteady they may be, however fragile in nature, however hesitant on the brink of nothingness, yet they do exist. However lax and weak they may be, even in their very being, they do exist.

I exist. However small I may be, I am. Respite is given to me and I enjoy it. Since the truth of the human condition is death, life is what must be explained. There is no tenancy nor lease without a proprietor. No hatchet is set on the root of a tree unless there is a woodcutter who brandishes it. There is no execution without an executioner. There is someone somewhere who is master over my death; it is to Him likewise that I owe my life and my being. They depend immediately upon Him. He is in constant possession of my death. It is He, then, who is in constant possession of my life. He can dismiss me; the fact is that I am never more than His visitor and guest. My life is but a breath. It is His own breath. All my strength is in His hand.

The master of life and death, sovereign owner of existence, who bestows it as He pleases, who withdraws it as He thinks fit, we call God. He is the ultimate reason for all, but only because there must be a reason. And, moreover, we are not very far ahead when we are constrained to acknowledge that He is the woodcutter who brandishes the hatchet, the supreme contradiction to all that is perishable. Because there must be an explanation, He is the sovereign explanation of our precarious existences. It is truly the opposite of a *deus ex machina* which intervenes only because the playwright is powerless to discover the natural ending of the plot. On the contrary, we discover God to be the center of the plot and the necessary ending for our own imbroglio. We discover in Him the immediate and Most High Lord of being and existence, He upon whose good pleasure each instant depends and without whom nothing would exist. Impossible not to be concerned about Him. The woman who does not wish to think of God hastens to join her lover—and she finds her lover dead. God is at home everywhere. Every place on earth, and my own place is a terrible place. It is the house of God, His domain and His property, and I did not know it.

My friend, what are you doing here?

And by a touch only of this sovereign hand the man dies. One might as well know at once where one stands. This universal seizure by God of everything that exists is indeed a truth more terrible than consoling. It is a brutal fact which imposes itself on everyone and on everything, and I do not claim it to be other than brutal. In this first stage of our reflection, we establish it rather as a servitude, a formidable presence at the origin of all being. It is no laughing matter. The main thing is to know how to accommodate oneself to this all-powerful grasp of the hand of God upon each one of us. Demons feel it

and tremble. Nothing is more cowardly than to wish
to ignore it. Many seek distraction from it, like the
bad Rich Man, and some defy it. The honest of mind
would, at the very least, recognize it.

★ ★ ★

Who has not, once in his life, experienced his de-
pendence and the fragility of existence? Who has not
at one time felt the anguish of being nothing and,
at the same time, the crushing weight of existing?
Who has not felt total powerlessness before the death
or betrayal by a loved one or before the menace of
his own death? Who has not felt the burning sensa-
tion of his own contingency, in the midst of one or
another of those bitter reflections which haunt the
meditation of Hamlet: ". . . the whips and scorns of
time, the oppressor's wrong, the proud man's con-
tumely, the pangs of disprized love, the law's delay,
the insolence of office, and the spurns that patient
merit of the unworthy takes, when he himself might
his quietus make with a bare bodkin"? Who has
never been deceived in his own sin? What detains
Hamlet on the border of suicide is the fear of an
irremedial deception.

If the world, this life, our being even, and death
also, deceive us, it is because something is lacking or
that our need is too vast, too demanding.

The world, ourselves, our life and our death: here
is the problem, the question of questions as Hamlet
so well saw. If the world and our own existence pose
no question for us, we have nothing to do with God.
But if we have the inexorable consciousness of the

absurdity of our condition, reduced to its base fac-
tors, and of the absurdity of the world as it presents
itself to our perception and our reflection, then, provided that we have the intellectual courage to force
the absurd to its very limits, to its fullest measure,
then alone are we close to the discovery that there
must necessarily be an intelligible complement to
this essentially deficient condition, a solution to the
absurd. This complement, this solution, this overflowing and mysterious answer, this ultimate reason
for all things, which is necessary without our knowing what it is, we call God. Nothing is more unpre-
tentious, more honest, more courageous, than this
process of the intelligence.

Modern philosophers cannot be reproached for
recognizing the absurdity of the world and of the
human condition: it is that even which traditional
philosophy calls contingency. They should be reproached for stopping short once they are on the
right road. At the end of absurdity there is necessarily a solution to absurdity, just as when one pur-
sues one's journey to the end of the night, one always
ends by emerging into the early morning. If one denies the necessity of a solution, the fact is that one
denies the problem as well. If the world is but absurdity then it would be totally so: cats would breed
dogs, a circle could be square, and a policeman's hel-
met would be filled with stars. There is no middle
course and one does make allowance for the absurd.
The world must either totally lack intelligibility or
be totally intelligible.

For, in a word, everything leads us back to that

starting point. There is too much intelligence in the world to permit it to be totally absurd. Absurdity itself is apportioned. And there is not enough intelligence in this world, in itself, for it to be its own sufficient reason for existing. It is too easy to proceed as if we were caught in this world and in this existence like flies on fly paper. Even from the point of view of the fly this sticky fate is but a fact, not an explanation. We are not very far advanced when we are told, in the language of Pascal or of Céline, that the world and our own existence are nothing more than booby traps. Progress has been made in becoming stupid, perhaps, but not in the rigorous discovery of reasons.

Obviously it is always possible to reject within ourselves the exigencies of the spirit. But does this not consist in denying ourselves and what makes us human? There, indeed, is the greatest abasement of man, this *pastime,* of which Pascal had such great horror, which prevents man from seeing himself as he is. "Thus man is so wretched that he would be bored without any cause of boredom, by the proper state of his disposition; and he is so vain that, being filled with a thousand essential causes of boredom, the least thing, like pushing a billiard ball, suffices to divert him."

The misfortune of man is to feel that ontologically he is not sufficient to himself. His misfortune consists in the fact that his attention is diverted from this view. His dignity demands that he face his misfortune and try to understand it. Confronting evil, confronting the essential boredom of his condition, con-

fronting the interior bewilderment of his contingency, the honor of man consists in saying to himself:
I will get to the bottom of it! Where do we come
from? Where are we going? Why are we so unhappy
here below?

When man has the courage not to let himself be
distracted from such questions, which have a bearing
on his whole destiny, then, and then only, does he
venture one day to make a breach in this prison of
the absurd in which he is enclosed, and to discover
God. Intelligence is not resignation, nor captivity.
It is liberty and revolt against the absurd, persistent
revolt. It is victory over the absurd. At the end of
this revolt the intelligence does not discover God as
a *problem* but as a *solution,* the sole valid solution
for its need of wholeness, the sole liberation.

At the threshold of this book I would like to en-
grave in the heart and in the mind of each of my
readers, with an acid and penetrating script, first and
foremost, this truth of theology: GOD IS NOT A PROB-
LEM. HE IS THE SOLUTION.

★ ★ ★

To what should be compared this discovery of God,
as the necessary and intelligible completion of ourselves and of the universe?

When all is said and done, what we indicate by
the name of God is the obscure other-worldly Being
who, in order that we may be able to understand
something of Him, *must* be the cause and the origin
of this world and of ourselves. Is it a discovery? Yes,
with respect to our frivolous and distracted nature,

which asks nothing more than not to pose problems to itself in order not to have to deal with inevitable and troublesome solutions.

Thus, the discovery of God can be compared to a *coup de théâtre*. The theater is made up of very crude stage devices but all depends on the genius of the author, not to mention the talent of the actors. Certain stage devices are classic but, well manipulated, are nonetheless effective. Thus, here and there in Shakespeare: A lad who in good faith thought he was the son of a shepherd suddenly discovers that he is a prince and son of a king. And then there is that horrible situation of a girl buried alive, who awakens in a burial vault near a corpse.

If one reflects upon it, the real and concrete situation of a man who for the first time discovers God, both as his origin and as his necessary companion, is more dramatic than any *coup de théâtre*. The thick veneer of our stupidity must scandalize the angels, for the very reason that ordinarily it does not upset us very much.

A young man, twenty years of age, who has always considered himself an orphan, discovers that his father is alive and that he can meet him, that he is even there among the crowd. The discovery of God is even more decisive. For, as a matter of fact, that child has lived without his father; the life which he has previously received from him, he maintains in his own right. Whereas at each instant we receive everything from this High Source, we live constantly in the bosom of the unknown matrix. If this bond uniting me to God were to break, I would return to nothingness.

This boy believed himself to be the son of a poor shepherd and it is revealed to him that he is the son of a king. The revelation of God is still more magnificent. All the majesties of the earth are as dust under His feet. Since He is the Source of all perfections of this world, He possesses them in Himself. But He possesses them in superabundance and in sublime brilliance. Heraclitus has said, "The most beautiful of apes is ugly if one compares it to humankind, and in respect to a God the most scholarly of men must seem like an ape."

But God, who is He in Himself? The fact that He is our supreme and total origin reveals nothing about Him. He is perfection, in all its fullness and depth. This fullness even isolates Him infinitely. God is of another world, however near He may be to every being by His creative power. He is there in the very heart of my being; but His presence is shadowy, formidable, as threatening as it is reassuring, and we perceive it only by groping for it. It is a revelation as mysterious and terrible as if I were to awaken suddenly at night in a tomb, bound in all my members to an unknown corpse. "That undefinable something which has no name in any language" is no more anguishing for man than "the King of Terror" who has a name in all languages.

Let all metaphysics, all theology, kneel and tremble before daring to look on this holy reality, holy and formidable, as secret as lightning, as deep as the heavens and the sea.

If the surgeon errs, his patient dies under his

hands. If the chemist does not conduct his experiment with minute precaution, he can explode with his laboratory. The discoverers of radium lost their lives in a horrible manner. If the construction engineer makes a false calculation, the trial pilot is destroyed in an immense burst of flame. No one has ever heard it said that God has struck down a simple theologian guilty of imprudence or inattention. And it is a real pity. Such an event would cause the profession to be taken more seriously. One should approach the subject of theology in love mingled with fear, in an attitude of penance and richly arrayed, as it is told of Queen Esther that she fasted three days with tears of grief and in prayer before clothing herself in all her glory in order to approach the king.

This admirable scene of the meeting of Esther with her king is the image of theological research. The queen leans on a handmaid and this companion is faith. A follower bears her train and this train-bearer is philosophy, literature, art, and all profane knowledge. Yes, one would dream that theology might be more timid than talkative, that she might have an exquisite understanding of demeanor and of those things capable of seducing the heart, and that she might have the strength not to speak until she felt the scepter on her neck, and the royal kiss on her lips.

"She, too, had recourse to the Lord in her fear of the danger that threatened. Laid aside were those royal robes of hers, her array must tell only of grief and lament; dust and dung should be all her anointing now. Her body she tamed with fasting; only her torn locks hung where once she had loved to adorn her beauty. In such guise she made her plea to the Lord. . . .

"When the third day came, she laid aside the garb of prayer, and put on all her fine array, queenly robes that dazzled the eye. One prayer she offered to the God who alone rules, alone can save; then bade two of her waiting-maids bear her company. On one she leant, as though her dainty form must needs be supported; the other followed her mistress as train-bearer. Alluring beauty of flushed cheek and shining eye hid a heart grief-stricken, a heart ready to swoon with fear. Door after door she passed, till she reached the king's presence, where he sat on his royal throne, royally clad, amid a glitter of gold and jewels; terrible of mien. No sooner had he looked up, his fiery glance betraying his angry humor, than the queen was ready to swoon away; white went her cheeks as she leaned her head, fainting, on the maid that stood by.

"And now God changed the king's mood all at once to mildness; he started from his throne in trembling haste, and was fain to hold her in his arms till she came to herself; and still with soothing words he reassured her: Esther, what is amiss with thee? Were I thy own brother, thou hadst not less cause to fear. Thy life is safe; to others the law forbids entry, never to thee; thou hast but to come near, and touch my scepter. And with that, for she was voiceless still, he raised his golden scepter and touched her neck with it; then kissed her and asked, What, hast thou no word for me? My lord, she said, the sight of thee overawed me, as if I had seen one of God's angels;

such reverence does thy majesty inspire. For indeed, my lord, there is nothing about thee but must be admired, nothing in thy looks but is gracious. Even as she spoke, once again her strength failed her, and she was near to fainting; the king was all anxiety, and his courtiers must needs come about him, seeking to allay her fears."

Theology should, first and foremost, be prayer. If it gain access to God, this can only be at the price of the outpouring of soul. And if intercourse with God is permitted, this can be only in the fear of deceiving such majesty. Wonderful privilege of that knowledge which transgresses forbidden frontiers: "To others the law forbids entry, never to thee."

We would like to explain the symbol of faith in the manner of St. Peter of Verona, who one morning put on his most handsome coat and had himself closely shaved, for, he said, he was invited to a wedding feast. He knew that he was going to die and he advanced on his way, singing, in the new light of an Easter morning. When he fell, struck on the head, he still had the strength to write with the hand which he dipped in his own blood, in large letters in the dust: CREDO.

Such are our masters, our brothers, our saints, the bodies fallen on the routes of the world; such is the ambition of our heart in the dust of words. And let him who passes stop suddenly, let him gaze on this evidence at his feet which bars his way. And may his soul be illuminated!

★   ★   ★

God is not a problem; He is the necessary and total solution of the problem posed by a universally absurd world. One does not compromise with the absurd. There is nothing here below which is not contingent, perishable, insufficient in itself. Even what does not die can be disintegrated, and the atomic bomb has conveyed to us the message that our hills are not eternal.

Not only every being, but all the perfections and interior resolves in being are not realized here below except in an insufficient and precarious manner. In all things and for all things, our accounts are short. I know well that in itself there is no reason that justice, for instance, or intelligence, or love, or liberty, should not be infinite. How does it happen that we always find them scandalously and sadly limited? Ah yes, our accounts are short, and in all our additions we lack the principal amount in order to reach the total, a sufficient and perfect sum.

Pascal is a very great genius. He has himself admirably explained that the order of intelligence surpasses the order of bodies by an infinite distance. Thought as such has no limit and its kingdom has no frontiers. Thought is free and sovereign, without obstacle or hindrance. Not even to mention death, it is absurd that the genius of Pascal was sometimes hindered by a migraine headache or simply by sleep. All human thought is weak. Hence it is not absolute thought. It also is absurd. It likewise needs to be explained and sustained by a thought that has no limits or lapses.

There must, then, be a solution even for human

thought, and this solution must be complete in its order. God cannot be a Being without consciousness; otherwise, everything must be begun all over again. A solution of the world which would be as indifferent to everything as a pebble would take no account of my thought, nor of its limit of weakness and anguish. My thought is solvable only in a spiritual Reality, which is to itself, in complete consciousness, its own inextinguishable flame and its own tranquillity. God is tranquil because He is absolute.

There would be no meaning in discovering an unconscious God. God must be primarily God-for-Himself. There would be nothing but shame for the intelligence to be obliged to defer to any unconscious being whatsoever. The unconscious cannot satisfy the intelligence. God is the Father of all enlightenment. There is no darkness in Him, no vicissitudes, no decline. He can be nothing other than transparency to Himself, and total generosity of the intelligence. "I am the Fire," He said to Catherine of Siena, "you are the sparks." All thought is lighted at His flame.

However free or powerful we may be, nomad in the desert or tyrant on a throne, we do not do everything that we will to do. And yet the notions of will, or power, or liberty, have no interior limits. A pure act of the will would be all powerful and its liberty infinite. It is absurd to will and not be able to effect what is willed, to will and not to pursue one's act to its completion, to be free and to be stopped by the least obstacle.

Oh, I do not speak of the fetters of morality, which certain persons take pride in breaking so that they

may definitely affirm their liberty. But the most absolute anarchist can be betrayed by his best friend;
he can suffer from it and I do not think that he would
do so freely. Were he even not to love anything or
anyone, in order to be more free, then he would
forgo loving, and in that he is no longer free. In any
case, he, too, is subject to vagaries. And his will becomes slack.

This congenital deficiency in the perishable being
thus contaminates all intelligence, all will, all liberty
here below. An absurd restriction not only of our being but of our thoughts and our love is a universal
scandal. We must then admit an ultimate reason not
only in the line of being but in the line of each of
the interior perfections of being, super-universal like
thought, will, liberty. . . . Everything which is af-
fected by absurdity and contingency has its immediate
origin in God. He is its superabundant origin and its
utmost cause.

We are naturally short in our accounts. If we include Him, and it is absolutely necessary to include
Him, we can close our books. He is the sum total of
being and that total is Unity, not in the manner of
arithmetical unity which does no more than begin
any sum, but a unity which is naturally the sum of all
being, the beginning and the end, the alpha and the
omega, the whole alphabet in Himself alone, and all
treatises do no more than repeat this indefinitely.

He is at one and the same time totality and unity
because He is the identity of the whole being and of
all super-universal perfections of being with being
itself. Far from disintegrating God in the cosmos as

pantheists lazily claim to do, it is His totality of being which makes up the ultimate differential cog of the Deity. God is infinitely distinguished from all other beings because He alone is all being in fullness and real depth.

Being in all the immense sweep of its intimate perfections, life, intelligence, love, and all their qualities, is summed up and crystallized in God in a unity so absolute that it is simplicity itself. Nothing is lacking in this excessive and serene simplicity; otherwise, He would be neither perfect nor total, He too would be contingent and restricted. Far from being the ultimate reason of all, He would still require justification.

I would like to say all this in a simpler manner, but it is impossible. It is difficult for our mind to conceive something about God. Our mind is naturally attuned to the essentially deficient intelligence of beings of our own level, that is, essentially deficient. God is nothing if He is not precisely the completion of this deficiency. In reality, when one tries to think of being in itself, it is easier to admit the existence of a being in natural plenitude of being. The scandal for the intelligence is that we may exist, restricted and parcelled out in being as we are. An intelligence which urges forward its intuition could never become accustomed to the existence of a limited being.

In His unity, vital simplicity, totality of being, in the lightning-quick and full consciousness of a sovereign and all-powerful intelligence, God appears to us fundamentally as a Person. This eminent personal-

ity is the seal of all His perfections, the absolute perfection of His simplicity and of His totalizing unity of
being. Each one of these perfections of being—and
He possesses all in an infinite degree since He is being in its absolute plenitude—is God in all simplicity, so that the name of each perfection is a divine
name: God is Spirit, He is Love, He is Liberty, He is
Justice. . . . And in all and for all, He is Someone.

This conclusion seems to me to be inevitable and
urgent, according to the needs of the spirit, not according to my natural desires. A pantheistic universe
would be more comfortable for me than this precipice beside me, this precipice, impossible to span naturally, between our sad world and this formidable
Presence, shadowy and all-powerful, in perfect con-
trol of Himself and of everything, including my life
and my death, this quiet Glance which follows me
without a flicker of the eyelid, and which judges me.
Fundamentally, I would prefer a God on my own level,
contained in the calyx of a flower or in a beloved
smile. It is absolutely not a matter of my tastes, it is
a matter of what is. This book is not a lyric poem, in
spite of the extraordinary vogue for lyricism in modern philosophy; it is a pursuit, galling as it may be,
of the truth.

These questions have all been made complicated,
as if for sheer pleasure of doing so—what pleasure?
I wonder. When one says of God that He is transcendent, that does not mean that He is beyond the clouds.
It means that He is here as an absolute sovereign of
being.

When one says that He is a perceptible being, that does not mean that He is manifest to us. It is true that He is light, but this Light is naturally only dimly accessible to us. In the natural order the universe is all vibrant with mysterious waves which we do not perceive or which we perceive only by the intermediary of delicate instruments. God is there in all His clarity, but as an Incomprehensible. It is within us that there is darkness. We are, in the presence of immense clarity, like wood-owls in broad daylight. Mystery is like a yoke on our feeble intelligence. God in Himself is Light alone!

We live and die in the presence of this Incomprehensible. "This sovereign personality," writes Maritain, "is what at the same time separates Him from us in the greatest degree—the inflexible Infinite face to face with a lowly man—and also brings Him nearest to us, since incomprehensible Purity has a countenance, a voice, and has put me before Him so that I may speak to Him and that He may answer. The light of His countenance has been fixed upon us: 'Why is it that Thou wilt make so noble a thing of man, wilt pay so much heed to him? Never a day dawns but Thou wilt surprise him at his post; never a moment when Thou art not making proof of him. Nay, gaze on me no more; leave me, though it were but for a breathing-space, to myself. . . . It was Thy hand that made me, no part of me but is Thy fashioning; and wilt Thou cast me aside? . . . It is to God, the omnipotent, I will speak. . . . O that my cause might be tried; that He, the Almighty, would grant my request, that He, my judge, would write my record down; how

proudly I would bear it with me, shoulder-high, wear
it as a crown!

" 'Then from the midst of a whirlwind, the Lord
gave Job His answer: Here is one that must ever be
clouding the truth of things with words ill-considered!
Strip, then, and enter the lists; it is My turn to ask
questions now, thine to answer them.' "

★ ★ ★

Man has two countries from which he derives
his origin, two native lands, and each one speaks to
him a different language: this world of problems
where the present existence of man is caught like a
rat in a trap, and another country, still unknown,
foreshadowed only, the kingdom of liberty and eternity where we will see things as they are and where
we ourselves will be understood.

> O Death, aged Captain, it is time, let us raise the anchor!
> This country wearies us, O Death! Let us get under way!
>   Sail on!

Philosophers and modern poets experience, to the
point where their heads swim, exasperation at the
contingency of the world and of themselves. "I was
furious that I had been brought into the world,"
writes Michel Leiris, "I revolted against the laws of
the universe, railed against gravity, resistance of matter, and the passing of the seasons. I did not exactly
and completely admit to myself that what loosed my
rage against life was not the condition which natural
and social laws have made for us, but simply death!"

I believe that I feel a like anguish. I know exactly
how to locate the point of the soul where this rage

rises only to become revolt. Each time I am tempted to shout "Bravo! *Toro!*" More often than not, I am disappointed to see the animal turn sharply and charge on the red cape, the great scarlet illusion of a subjective and momentary solution. In reality, everyone recognizes perfectly well that for absurdity there must be the solution of a Creator, an Almighty God. Each one claims to assume the role personally and pretends to reign as a master in the celestial Jerusalem of artificial paradises.

"If you are not to be the martyred slaves of Time," wrote Baudelaire, "become drunk!" St. Paul also had this idea about time which he found too short in every respect, and also about an ever-changing world. He desired for man another kind of drunkenness. "Do not besot yourselves with wine . . . let your contentment be in the Holy Spirit!" It is a pity to replace the true God by drugs and to be satisfied with an ersatz eternity. André Breton can well write: "One must have done with time, that sinister old trickster." While Breton is not Joshua in person, this metaphysical revolt is nothing other than a sentimental news item and, from the moment that it issues forth only in automatic language, it is dream and poetry.

We knew all that. It recalls to us certain promises which have been made to us. We await the messenger who will proclaim in a voice resounding from one end of the universe to the other, that there is no more time. Enough pleasantries. We have already been warned that there is no sacred threshold other than death: "None can see God without dying."

We cannot meet God and see Him without dying, but can He meet us and join us? Certainly He can do so, since His personality, sovereignly intelligent and free, is also all-powerful. But it is He who must come the whole way to meet us. That we may not die, He will have to come all the way to us with human steps, not according to His way but according to ours, under the mask of enigma and as in a mirror.

"Moses . . . drove the flock to the inner parts of the desert, and came to the mountain of God, Horeb. And the Lord appeared to him in a flame of fire out of the midst of a bush: and he saw that the bush was on fire and was not burnt.

"And Moses said: I will go and see this great sight, why the bush is not burnt.

"And when the Lord saw that he went forward to see, He called to him out of the midst of the bush, and said: Moses, Moses. And he answered: Here I am.

"And He said: Come not nigh hither, put off the shoes from thy feet: for the place whereon thou standest is holy ground.

"And He said: I am the God of thy father, the God of Abraham, the God of Isaac, and the God of Jacob. Moses hid his face: for he durst not look at God. . . .

"Moses said to God: Lo, I shall go to the children of Israel, and say to them: The God of your fathers hath sent me to you. And if they should say to me: What is His name? what shall I say to them?

"God said to Moses: I AM WHO AM. . . . Thou shalt say to the children of Israel: HE WHO IS hath sent me to you."

It is He, and not another, who really comes to us, the God of Abraham, of Isaac, and of Jacob, but who is at the same time the God of all wisdom and all knowledge. When He speaks His name, it is indeed His mysterious identity which He discloses. But He uses our words, He speaks in our language, He makes Himself understood by us. The words which He pronounces—and He does pronounce them—are earthly words. Such is the style of all Divine approaches here below. It is also a human hand which God extends to save us, human, so very human, that we run the risk of not acknowledging it as the hand of salvation. Whoever understands this, understands the typical style of religion, that ambiguity of Christianity in which everything that represents God here below contains God authentically, and His very substance or His intelligence, but under appearances and in an expression which remain inadequate because they remain human.

But it is up to us, led by Him, to take the return path. It is well worth while to use all the courage of our intelligence and to penetrate through the human words to the meaning of this holy language. There is one way to say all this: God had REVEALED Himself. The discovery and knowledge of this universe beyond the world are henceforth accessible to us.

There is a whole tradition of modern writers which endeavors to come to the point of blaspheming against God. This is what I call the architecture of false windows. They wish to lay claim not only to gifts like miracles and prophecy, but to the most personal privileges of God, like revelation and grace, sanctity, and especially creative omnipotence. They want to be seers, wonderworkers of words, and prophets imbued with grace and sanctity in opposition to God. They know perfectly well that to accomplish this, they must transcend human means. They know very well that they must purify the language and that there is no remission of sins without the shedding of blood. They know all this. They accept it, including the redeeming sacrifices, provided that God be eliminated. All that has no meaning except through God. But God must be profaned, despoiled not only of His attributes, but also of His majesty, even of His personality. He must be alienated from Himself and rendered mad. It is we who are mad!

May at least the heroism of these sacrilegious attempts restore to Christians the lofty meaning of the greater good which has been given to them. The revelation of God in the life of each man who takes it seriously, at its true value, is a heart-rending event. To say that the mode of expression of this revelation remains human and that its content is authentic, sacred, supernatural, and divine, is an exact and classic theological formula. When in the exercise of knowledge, intelligence does conform to that formula, it can only be by purity and the obedience of total sacrifice. There are also holocausts of the mind.

The threshold which leads to God is death. There is a death and a resurrection of the intelligence which accede to the revelation of a living God and it must indeed be so, since God is beyond the world. But it must also be God Himself who gives us the strength to face this agony of mind without flinching and without losing ourselves in the shadows. "What though I walk with the shadow of death all around me? Hurt I fear none, while Thou art with me." Yes, it is You and not another, my Lord and my God.

★ ★ ★

"The last approach of reason," says Pascal, "is to recognize that there is an infinite number of things which surpass it. It is but weak, if it does not go that far. If natural things surpass it, what must one say of the supernatural?" We can know only by Revelation the most lofty reality, the richest intelligibility, and the infinite domain of the intimate nature of God. We know that God exists, but who is He? I know also that passerby whom I see from my window; he exists but I do not know who he is. I could perhaps become his friend. I would have to approach him, he would have to speak to me. It is too late. He has already passed by irrevocably. Everyone knows what I mean. Everyone keeps in his memory a few faces, radiant and unforgettable, which he allowed to pass by.

Shall we permit the opportunity of knowing God to pass? To pose the principle that we must deprive ourselves of all communication with the Divine world which dominates us would be still more absurd than to refuse to know the sensible world which we dominate. No one puts out the eyes of new-born babies. That is also why, in the Catholic Church, they are baptized. To be sure, this Divine world is still richer, more nourishing to the intelligence, still more beautiful, vast, and surprising than the world which we see. The least vestige of this knowledge is more precious than all the other sciences put together.

How can we explore this Divine world? We do not have access to it straightway. Certainly, by analogy we can, so to speak, encircle its reality and its connections. There is a natural theology, but it is sparse. God speaks. He has spoken. He has revealed the secrets of His life. We can know Him and enter into intimacy with Him. We have but to submit our intelligence into His keeping. "Submission and use of reason," says Pascal, "are what constitutes true Christianity. There is nothing which conforms so closely to reason as this disavowal of reason." And moreover, it is much less disavowal than a confident heightening of this reason. The most lofty *rationabile obsequium,* reasonable docility, the most noble use of our reason, consists in bending it to the keeping of God, to open it to His supernatural light and to ponder His revelation.

God has spoken once and for all, and His revelation is transmitted to us. Joinville, the historian of St. Louis, will support my words: "He [St. Louis] said that faith and belief were one thing in which we should believe all the more firmly, since we are certain of it only by hearsay. On this point he asked me my father's name and I told him that he was called Simon. And he asked me how I knew it. And I told him that I thought I was certain of it and believed it firmly because my mother had borne witness to it. Then he said to me: So should you believe firmly all

the articles of faith to which the Apostles bear witness
as you hear them sung in the *Credo* on Sunday."

To be sure, St. Louis is right. It is the testimony of
the Apostles which transmitted the revelation of God
to us, and it is because our knowledge of God depends
on a testimony that it is a faith. "And the Word was
made flesh," said St. John, "and came to dwell among
us; and we had sight of His glory, glory such as belongs
to the Father's only-begotten Son, full of grace and
truth. . . . We have all received something out of
His abundance. . . . No man has ever seen God; but
now His only-begotten Son, who abides in the bosom
of the Father, has Himself brought us a clear message." Thus, by the Apostles and through them, it is
to the Man-God that we give credit, as the Apostle St.
Paul likewise affirms: "When we delivered the divine
message to you, you recognized it for what it is,
GOD'S MESSAGE, not man's."

Some consider these intermediaries and this recourse unworthy of reason which is critical and needs
evidence. Let us go slowly. There is, nonetheless, another domain which is immense, and which our age
prides itself on having explored to a greater extent,
and which likewise depends on hearsay and, consequently, on faith. It is the history and the past of humanity. It would be folly to contest the authenticity
of this knowledge which is likewise based on the
transmitted document, on eye-witness accounts, and
on sources. I shall be told that historical knowledge
criticizes its sources. But our faith also criticizes its
sources and makes just as many demands. In the
Church we find exegesis, the history of dogmas, and

commentaries on theology. For some people they take on so much importance that they would be tempted to stop all theology at this point, like children play at going to Siberia with three chairs in a parlor. But after a strict criticism of sources, eye-witness accounts, documents, it seems to us as honorable for human reason to believe in the Trinity as to believe in the reality of the Treaty of Westphalia. Our religion is straightforward indeed! Are we not more honest in admitting that our knowledge of God and His revelation is based on faith than those who confer on history the perfect dignity of science?

It is true that the domain of history remains on our level and is an object of natural faith. It is only *in fact* that it is directly incommunicable to us, because of the succession of time which localizes us narrowly in a given moment. On the other hand, it is *by right* that we are naturally incapable of knowing the intimacy of God, because the life of God infinitely surpasses the normal means of investigation of our intelligence. The line of our historical research and of our knowledge of the past remains horizontal, on man's level. I could have been present at the battle of Gettysburg; I could have seen it. For the historical machine, there is no shift for reaching back in time. The line of our divine faith and of our supernatural knowledge is vertical. No one has at any time seen God but the One who has brought us His message. The knowledge of supernatural faith raises us and sustains us constantly above ourselves; it infinitely surpasses the impetus of all created intelligence. One reaches God only through grace. As it is said of Queen Esther:

"To others the law forbids entry, never to thee." Every intelligence other than the one enlightened by grace stops before the threshold.

Above all, faith is a grace, namely, a gift of God. The natural light of our mind suffices to make us understand that two and two make four and that Washington crossed the Delaware. These are truths which we can understand. But the truth of God is so concealed in us and above us, that we need a special intuition, a supernatural light infused in our hearts by God Himself. This light is gratuitous and depends on God alone, who gives it to whom He will. It does not depend on our natural gifts. God is the sum of the intelligence, and the genius of Aristotle is infinitely small before Him. A poor, unlettered beggar woman who has the faith is richer than Aristotle in knowledge of God, because the light which she possesses is from God.

Those who possess this light have it stored up, a secret flame, active in the winds of passion and the night of exile. It enables them to judge the world and life from inside as God sees them. They know what is behind appearances. When I drive beside a plowed field, I do not know what it will yield. The farmer who has sown it knows that he can count on barley or wheat the next summer. Thus, this light of faith in our souls is the token and the beginning of eternity. It guides us to the point where God Himself, in the manifestation of His glory, will rise up on every side to meet us like the overwhelming coming of the dawn; without ever having seen Him before, we will recognize Him so clearly that it will seem to us that this tremendous jubilation has its birth in our own hearts.

Faith is a grace; that is why it solicits and engages our liberty. It is a gift; we can refuse it or beg for it. It is a trust which we place in God. But we know Him whom we trust. From the standpoint of honor, God is a gentleman. He has but one word and He has given it to us.

★ ★ ★

"One must know when to doubt, when to affirm," says Pascal, "and when to submit. He who does not act accordingly does not understand the power of reason. There are those who fail against these three principles in affirming everything as demonstrable because they do not know the rules of demonstration; or in doubting everything because they do not know the rules of submission; or in submitting in everything; they do not know where they must judge."

★ ★ ★

What, then, is faith? Generally it is a mode of knowledge, and at first it is a very imperfect mode of knowledge which, however, can include certitude, not only subjective certitude, but also a certitude which is perfectly assured in objective reality.

There is no perfect mode of knowledge except evidence. Certitude is inherent in this perfect method. It is thus that in the sensible order we have the evidence of light, and in the intellectual order the evidence of first principles. We know very well that we cannot, at the same time and with the same being, affirm and deny the same thing in the same connection. If a cap is white, it cannot be black. A metaphysician has the intuition of the being which is the basis of his certainty. The scientific method, which in departing from evident principles extends the certainty of this evidence to the extreme conclusions of science, is equally sure.

In our knowledge of the mystery of God, evidence momentarily escapes us. Angels and saints in paradise have evidence of God because they see Him face to face and their glorified intelligences immediately quench their thirst at this blessed source of all light. We, here below, know God only *through hearsay*. What can be the degree of certainty of such knowledge and what is its nature?

When knowledge does not derive its origin and its legitimacy from evidence, it cannot be completed and consummated with certainty on the level of intelligence. There must be an intervention of the will or of the passions to make us decide. Thus, there may be *suspicion:* in that case the certainty of the intelligence results from the fact that it makes a choice of one of two conclusions that face it, but base this only on slight and perhaps meaningless evidence. There could not be certainty except in a deceptive way, the certainty of Othello. Again, the intelligence can reach a conclusion and at the same time retain the fear that the contrary conclusion might be the true one: in that case the conclusion is simply an *opinion*. Finally, when the intelligence fails to reach a decision between two possible conclusions, then there is *doubt*.

Essentially, faith does not admit of suspicion and doubt, and it is not an opinion. I am certain that the Roman Empire existed. Faith has this in common with suspicion, doubt, and opinion, that, like them, it is not based on evidence. It is based mainly on testimony. But it is an assurance and a firm adhesion of the intelligence, determined by the will, without any trouble or disturbance, by reason of the authority of the testimony. Such is perfect faith.

We must be careful to note that a simple opinion and sometimes suspicion are expressed by the verb *to believe*. There is a very different degree of assurance in my mind when I say, on one hand, I believe they are lying to me, or I believe that it will rain tomorrow; or, on the other hand, I believe that Louis XIV was king of France and that Joan of Arc was burned at Rouen.

In the first two cases, there are suspicion and an opinion in which certainty is far from being assured. In the latter case, although I do not know Louis XIV or of the suffering of Joan of Arc except by testimony, it is certainty which I express. Thus, we do not say commonly, I believe that Washington was the first president of the United States; but rather, so certain our belief appears to us, I know that Washington was the first president of the United States.

So, when we say according to the Catholic faith, that Jesus is God, it is more than an opinion which we express. It is a certainty. We could as well say, I am *certain*, or I know, that Jesus is God.

The Catholic faith is a firm and certain assent to one truth which is proclaimed to us without fear of error. To the extent that our faith is mixed with doubt arising from temptation or from our mediocrity, it is not perfect. Too often we hear the Christian religion discussed, even by believers and even in the pulpit, not in the tone of certainty, but rather expressed as an opinion, timidly and without the solemn assurance of unmixed truth: "As if it were true"— with the courteous discretion that one uses in advancing what actually would be but an opinion. Whereas even in refined society we need use no oratorical precaution when we say that Washington was the first president of the United States or that the battle of Lexington was fought in 1775. It would be a laughing matter if one spoke of these things with caution, just as we must make the angels laugh, if angels can laugh.

Subjectively we are so sensitive to evidence and the direct sight of things that, like the Apostle Thomas, we always prefer to see in order to believe. But objectively, the Catholic faith is still more certain than any human knowledge and the evidence of the senses. In science the cause for certainty is the avidity of human reason for evidence. In the Catholic faith the cause of certitude is the light of God which infuses our intelligence and raises us up to Him, and it is the truth of God to which our mind adheres and which is most necessary and most permanent. God is not lying, not dreaming, and His language is sure.

Thus, beyond the teaching of the Church, beyond the testimony of the Apostles, and through them, it is in God whom we believe, God who has given us His word as a man of honor gives his word that what he affirms is true. *Et honni soit qui mal y pense.* God has given us His Word, His Son, the eternal and living fruit of His intelligible glory, the Word which has completed all prophecies and which is the principle of all the testimonies of the martyrs and Apostles. The authenticity of this document is sealed by the blood of the Cross. Pascal believed witnesses who allowed themselves to be killed in support of their beliefs. But He is the first witness who underwent death in order to give His testimony. Our faith drips with His blood. Christ, then, is at the center of our faith. He is its object, for He is the Truth, the first Truth in Person, the Word inscribed in the flesh, as its witness and its guarantee, for it is through Him, through His testimony, through His martyrdom, that our faith attains God: He is the Way; it is in Him also that our intelligence finds, even here below, its most certain accomplishment and its highest life.

★ ★ ★

Why would the intelligence of man escape the general law that the inferior adds to its perfection through its union with the superior? A wild rose remains essentially what it is but it is more beautiful for having become a rosebush under the hand of the gardener. A beautiful marble remains marble, but its destiny is a glorious one when it has fallen into the hands of Praxiteles or of Maillol. A dog's extreme familiarity with its master can confer on him a kind of like spirit. Puck, Giradoux's dog, showed the whimsy of his master. At the latter's death, he became stupid again; he no longer had anything to reflect. A woman in love betrays in her eyes, repeats in the intonations of her voice, the distinction or the baseness of the man she loves. The overwhelming lucidity of the saints, the replies of Joan of Arc, make us see the quality of perfection that flowers in the intelligence of man through intimate knowledge of God. The saints are never stupid. And what is astonishing is the fact that a man's commerce with God, a long and living familiarity with Him, can endow him with a sharper and more universal intelligence, and incline him to the ways and courtesy of his royal Friend?

We must then learn to know God. And since naturally we do not perfectly comprehend what He is in Himself, we must, first of all, have confidence in Him, accept His revelations and try to understand His teaching, place ourselves in His school. Truly, what a strange idea to think that faith can make a slave of our intelligence! Nonetheless, the point of view of God in regard to Himself and in regard to the world which He has created seems interesting. To have known Bonnard or Bernanos personally and to have heard what they themselves thought about their art and about life has never seemed to lessen their stature for me. On the contrary, to have known them has been of great help in understanding their work. But the work of God is the universe and ourselves. If He really has something to say about it, I will listen with all my ears.

The story is classic, much more simple than one thinks. There comes to my mind the way in which a young missionary set out for China. He did not know Chinese. On the boat he had the good fortune to make the acquaintance of a man who had spent all his life in China and who spoke the language admirably. The young missionary set about learning from this man, and first of all he believed him because his whole conversation was filled with proofs. Nothing is more reasonable than this act of faith. What would we say about this young missionary if he constantly contradicted his generous teacher regarding the form of a word or the turn of a sentence? On arriving in China he was, on the contrary, happy to have been amenable, to have allowed himself to be initiated into the language and customs of those among whom he must spend his entire life.

We have embarked toward another celestial kingdom, our eternal home. On our boat, if there are some who know the mysterious language of this distant country, how quickly we will seek information from them, what good students we will be, what an effort we will make to remember the meanings of the words of the native language which we have forgotten! We will want to know this language so that we may not be too alien when we reach our fatherland and, at least so that doors may not be closed against us as against strangers.

How difficult everything seems! To know God, must we make long and arduous studies, enter an advanced institute of Oriental language? Let us be reassured! The apprenticeship of God is accessible to all; we have been initiated by baptism and the language of faith is everyone's language. It is the common language which reflects another meaning, a meaning hidden from the profane. It is a mysterious language, but its secret is the secret of love. For, above theologians, through the teaching of the Church and the testimony of the Apostles, it is God Himself, who for each of us is the Schoolmaster, the Doctor of all men, who speaks to the heart.

It is a little like a young woman who has married a foreigner and who learns the language of the one whom she loves, or like the child who tries to understand his nurse. What makes everything easier is, above all, the complicity of life. When two beings love one another, the same words that everyone uses sometimes take on an added significance, known to them alone. It frequently happens in a large family that this complicity of a secret language contained within ordinary words keeps out the "barbarian." This is usually accomplished by outbursts of laughter within the family which others do not understand. The Church is a numerous family, and if our faith were living we would often feel like laughing in connivance with the Good Lord. The Gospel, read by a believer, is understood from the interior. The infidel remains without. "This law is not made for thee, but for all others."

Our speech with God is that of love because the apprenticeship of God is the apprenticeship for our final happiness. Our intelligence is called upon to contemplate God face to face, just as the eye is made for light. God, the First Truth, is also the Sovereign Good, that in which everything is brought into harmony, that truth without which everything misfires. There is no glory in being something without God. If one feels oneself without God and His light, if one is in "outer darkness," according to the terrible expression of the Gospel, still one must try to return to the grace of this light. That is the great endeavor of which Pascal speaks.

He says of unbelievers: "If they are regretful in the depths of their hearts that they have no more light, let them not dissimulate it; this declaration would not be at all shameful. There is no shame except in not being ashamed. Nothing marks an extreme weakness of intelligence more than not recognizing the misfortune of a man without God. Nothing marks more clearly a bad disposition of heart than not to desire the truths of the eternal promises. Nothing is more cowardly than to simulate bravado against God. Let them, then, leave these blasphemies to those who are of such low origin as to be truly capable of them. Let them be at least honest if they cannot be Christians, and let them recognize that there are two kinds of persons that one can call reasonable: either those who serve God with all their hearts because they know Him, or those who seek Him with all their hearts because they do not know Him."

II

RETURNING TO GOD

Translated by
ALASTAIR GUINAN

CHRISTIANITY has opened to the world the possibility of a personal love of God, as well as revealing the supernatural quality of that love; and it has taught men to express their love for God in those two givings of oneself which we call love of neighbor and prayer. It is in these two ways that the characteristically Christian manner of loving God expresses itself; and we may indeed know that the love which stirs within us comes from God if it moves us to concern ourselves with our brethren as well as to pray.

The chief commandment given to us by Jesus, the only one which displays the measure of His love, is this: "Thou shalt love the Lord thy God with the love of thy whole heart, and thy whole soul, and thy whole mind, and thy whole strength." It is not the precept itself which is new—for that, indeed, existed under the Old Dispensation—the *newness* lies in the fact that this commandment may be considered as sufficient in itself; it is, as it were, an assurance of the very substance of religion. Jesus declared that the keeping of this commandment sums up in itself all acts of true religion and embraces all the obligations of a true servant of God. On the other hand, a life externally rich in practices of devotion, but lack-

ing the love of God required by this commandment
and its dual implementation in prayer and in love of
neighbor, will be a mockery of Christian living, an
existence without supernatural substance, a mere appearance of the reality it counterfeits.

There probably does not exist even one Christian
who has not at some time in his life really desired to
love God, wholeheartedly and in such a way that sep-
aration from Him would be impossible. *Be no longer
a stranger to me, O Lord!* How many times has this
kind of love of God been loyally sought and asked for
in a prayer battering with bold confidence at the por-
tal of that Sacred Heart who is the King and Center of
all hearts! Yet, it often enough transpires that the
petitioner feels that he has not been heard, or even
that he has been strangely thrown back upon himself.
Still, God does not deceive us; and we know the
words of the Gospel: "If any one of yourselves is
asked by his son for bread, will he give him a stone?
If he is asked for a fish, will he give him a serpent
instead? Why, then, if you, evil as you are, know
well enough how to give your children what is good
for them, is not your Father in heaven much more
ready to give wholesome gifts to those who ask Him?"

This text must be read and re-read. So solemn a
promise is not one to be broken. It would be blas-
phemous to think of God as being more wanting in
heart than the best of men, and there is no man so
inhumane as to offer a serpent to his own son who,
in hunger, had sought food from his father. Howsoever wretched a man may be, it is not to be thought
that God will fail to give him His love, if he claim it

on the strength of God's own promise and on the fact
of being himself a child of God. It is impossible that
God, unless He had less heart than the most unlov-
ing of men, would disregard His own word in such an
instance. Therefore, we must come before Him and
say to Him yet again: "I am Your most unworthy
child, but nevertheless Your child. I beg of You Your
love, for I need it more than I need my daily bread.
I will never stop asking You until You hear me."

Many are they who, at one time or another, have
said this. Many there are who have given themselves
to prayer most wholeheartedly, even violently, and
sometimes heroically. They have set out to seek the
face of God, knowing that apart from Him their lives
will be dull and empty, useless, and not worth the effort of mere survival. And it has seemed to such men
that if they were to meet God face to face—perhaps
in the darkness of night, but nonetheless truly—even
once, even for a moment, their lives would be
entirely re-established, revitalized, and touched anew
with divine meaningfulness. Now, an electric cable is
charged so highly that merely to touch it is to risk a
shock, and God is a Being more powerful than the
thunderbolt, a Living Being so vital and animating
that our souls need only the slightest contact with
Him to be charged with love as from the fiery furnace
of charity. It cannot be thought that such contact will
fail to renew life and to transfigure the spirit.

Still, it may be that after much striving nothing
has happened. The soul continues in a state of spiritual lethargy; and when it measures the slightness
of the love which it senses, by the multifarious efforts

it has made, it seems as though it has been deceived and God has failed in His promise. Such a soul turns back into itself in all the dejection of disappointment, turning away from God because it appears that God has not wished to bend down toward it.

And the truth is that the most necessary of all elements has been wanting. The tiniest little bit of insulation can interfere with an electric current and make contact impossible. The soul may think it has done much to draw near to God, when in reality there has always been between it and Him an obstacle, perhaps very tiny, even one so slight as not to be perceived, yet big enough to cause the soul to be cut off from God. Contact has not been made. It is as though there had been set up some great electrical apparatus, but no provision had been made for the initial contact which would unite it to the source of electric energy, so that current might flow through all the wires of the apparatus, lighting all the lamps and warming all the radiators that depended upon it. There are many who seem to be leading really Christian lives but who are actually like such electrical installations, rich in possibilities but wanting in that current which will vitalize them: the current of God's love touches them not at all. We need have only a very small lamp; yet, if it be truly in contact with the source of current, it will give a real light. So our souls must remain always in contact with the true source of light.

It is just this moment of contact that I would describe, together with its underlying conditions, and the way in which prayer can bring it about.

My professor of chemistry was a fine fellow, and he spoke with eloquence. He would say before one of his experiments: *Let us put two substances in the presence of each other,* using, for example, sulphuric acid and copper. This is, in fact, a sort of ritualistic formula with chemists, and they are accustomed always to preface their experiments with such words, just as most of the prayers in the catechism classes begin with the similar formula: *Let us place ourselves in the presence of God.* Now, both these expressions have the same meaning; and the first of them, which concerns chemical reactions, will help us to understand the second, which has to do with prayer. My chemistry professor would in fact combine action with words, and when he said "Let us place sulphuric acid and copper in the presence of each other," he would take the sulphuric acid from its place on the shelf, do likewise with the copper, and then make ready to mix them. On the other hand, many a Christian says, "Let us place ourselves in the presence of God," and often does nothing of the sort: he is satisfied to leave God where He is; and he himself does nothing to try to turn to God. Under such conditions, it is certain that the net result will be exactly nothing, for no confrontation of the soul with God can take place. The first, most necessary, condition of prayer is *to place oneself in the presence of God.*

In order to do this—to effect contact with God—it is vitally important to consider who God is and in what way one is to turn to Him. Now God is not a created being; on the contrary, it is He who has made all things. He is entirely outside the circle of crea-

tion, transcending it completely. We might run over
the whole earth and never encounter the face of God.
He is infinitely beyond it all. We cannot reach, measure, or grasp Him, as we can when we hold a created
thing. *We must go beyond all this.* By so much as we
are taken up with any created thing, whatever it may
be, we are not really concerned with God. I am now
using these expressions in their most concrete sense.
When I say that God ought to occupy our thoughts, I
mean it just as I would speak of *occupying a territory
or a house.* Prayer will have reached its true state if
God fills us just as a camper takes possession of his
tent. Contact with Him will be at its maximum and,
so to speak, realized in every part. It becomes an indwelling of God in us.

Therefore, if I allow created things to fill my mind
while I am praying, it is with them that I am filled;
and God, not being a created thing, will be far off
from me. He is not, of course, to be thought of as
being with me in the unique sense in which He inheres in Himself. He can be with me, however, by
His grace; but when I am more taken up with others than with Him, it is not He alone who concerns me.
Under such conditions there is no real intimacy; for
like ourselves, as much as He loves us, He will never
reveal his secrets except when He is alone with us.

This putting of ourselves into the presence of God,
which is a gateway to all true prayer, can be compared
to temptation. In temptation what happens is that we
have to determine whether we will turn aside from
God in order to attach ourselves, *by preference,* to a
created thing. In prayer what happens is that we must
decide whether we will turn to God as He is in Him-

self. The condition of this decision becoming actual is that we must be detached, for at least a moment, *from everything but God Himself*. One may perfectly well be attached to more than one created thing at the same time: they are not always incompatible among themselves, and it frequently happens that they mutually complement one another. Consequently, one can occupy oneself with several of them without confusion and for the love of God. But at the very instant that we seek to turn to God, as He is in Himself, we must realize that He is perfectly sufficient unto Himself, and that He cannot be a mere third party. Inasmuch as He is the completeness of perfection, He completes all things. From the instant that we determine to put ourselves in His presence, the prime thing to do is to take account of this unique quality in Him, to pay it the homage of the soul's total reverence, by ignoring all others and all else, just as if a king were passing by.

It is true, of course, that the road over which the king passes was made for all to traverse, and that we must ourselves be concerned with the thousand occupations of life: but at the moment the king goes by, the road seems to have been made only for him. When we pray, let us properly prepare the road into our hearts, seeing to it that all created things are kept out of the line of march. It is a matter, first of all, of doing honor to God. God is a sovereign so mindful of His own dignity that if He does not find way made for Him into our hearts, He is not likely to enter at all. Or rather, it is we ourselves who will not recognize Him, because He will be lost in the crowd.

The first effort, then, that we must make in prayer

is like the effort we make in resisting temptation. In temptation it seems that our sensibilities, our imagination, all the lower inclinations of our will are drawn toward something which will separate us from God, if we consent to attach ourselves to that thing. But the apex of the will retains, at whatever cost, its firm hold upon God. The full faithfulness of the soul plants itself upon a narrow summit of the will to reveal itself by an almost despairing *No,* as though it finds only treason in the promptings of nature. This *No* prevails; and by means of it our faithfulness to God is maintained. In prayer, something analogous takes place; but here the plan of action is very much broader. Now it is not simply that a morally base object is set before us. It is now every created thing that interposes between the self and God, and that we must overpass if we are to find Him where He is. The great difficulty in this matter arises from a want of carefulness on our part. On the pretext that things which come into our mind can be neither bad nor forbidden, we readily believe that we are not in the wrong when we dwell upon them even while we are at prayer: it is thus that we are led astray. In reality we never actually come to the point of placing ourselves in the presence of God.

Always between God and ourselves there stands the barrier of created things, diverting us from the actuality of His presence. The most dangerous of such obstacles, *judged from this point of view,* are not even the things which might be to us occasions of sin, for we know once and for all that we must detach ourselves from these or else abandon God; but, rather, they are those created things that we are bound to love and even to love very much. Such are indeed the most dangerous obstacles in the act of prayer; for they are themselves distinct from God, and they more than other things prevent us from entering whole-heartedly into His presence. It is all very true to say that there is no sin in thinking of them; but the whole issue that concerns us is: *Do we really wish to open ourselves to God?* Then, it is all the more neces-sary that we push all such things out of the way for the time, all the more especially because they are in themselves good and harmless to us. This is the rea-son why St. Catherine of Siena, who of all others had a most refined understanding of the meaning of friendship, advised Raymond of Capua to turn aside from every created thing, and from herself the first of all. She nonetheless loved Raymond very much, and he remained devoted to her until the end of his life; yet at the time of prayer the least one can do is to give oneself up solely to God. Coming into God's presence, intimate union with Him—these are bought at such a price.

Prayer is the very highest act of valor, and it needs an impetus which ceaselessly spurs on the whole of one's being. An old axiom of the French cavalry ex-horts us *to cast our hearts beyond the obstacle that confronts us,* and adds immediately that *our horses will then leap forward to reach it.* In our case the ob-stacle is the entire universe, the whole of creation. We must therefore project our hearts to the utmost limit, beyond the very summit of heaven.

Prayer is the very shadow of death spread over our

hearts. *What though I walk with the shadow of death all around me? Hurt I fear none, while Thou art with me.* God is with us only at the price of our willingness to walk, first of all, through the fearsome shadow of death. One comes before God as one who has died. Death is to give up one's soul. Prayer is turning the soul aside from oneself and from all else, in order to give it into the hands of Him of whom St. Paul has written: "It is a fearful thing to fall into the hands of the living God." This is indeed the time to marshal all one's courage, as a little boy of six who said to me, "I will never fall back." And when I asked, "Are you never afraid? "Oh yes," he said, "I am afraid. But then I go forward!"

Prayer is really the shadow of death; it shares all its appearances and all its exactions. Christians have long been accustomed to say of one who dies, "He is gone before God." How like this is the other expression, "Let us place ourselves in the presence of God." The ancient Jews saw this rightly when they declared that no man could see God without dying. Truly, no one enters into the presence of God unless he first dies. That withdrawal from all created things which is death is foreshadowed by the withdrawal which prayer requires. All that one has must be left behind, possessions, friends, even the very dearest of them; even the body itself must be forgotten as it grows cold and the soul slips out of it; the very soul, indeed, must be delivered into the hands of the unknown; it must plunge deeply into the dizzying abyss of the beyond: this we call death. I think that it is so also that we must pray; and in praying we must freely make up our minds to give up all these things: we must turn our hearts away from all we cherish, just as death forces us to do. If the saints find it easier to die than do others, it is because they have been for so long habituated to pray with all their hearts. They have, as we might say, become practiced in dying; and to do it once more is very easy.

It is as easy, or as difficult as one wishes, to pray as it is to die. The kingdom of God suffers violence: it is taken by those who storm it. The great majority of men prefer, at whatever cost, to spare themselves this violent uprooting of the self from all its attachments. Many are more ready to spend whole nights at the bedsides of the sick than to face unreluctantly, and with all the generosity and self-sacrifice which it entails, the task of making the effort which will put them in the presence of God. This, nevertheless, is what is demanded of us; and there are two sorts of souls in our world. There are those who pray, and there are those who pray not at all or so badly that they never detach themselves from the idols of their hearts even during the moments when they are at prayer. Such souls are at the mercy of this world which they never want to be quit of.

Clearly, this is a hard saying. And this is all the more reason for emphasizing such prayer. If we are to experience pleasure in praying, if it is to bring with it a joyous and intimate savor, it may be that man does not know whether he prays that he may come closer to God, or simply for his own pleasure and personal satisfaction; for the joy of prayer is dear to the heart and requites it for many a sacrifice. But when prayer offers no sensible satisfaction of any sort, when it seems to bring in its train nothing but dryness and a kind of dark despair, if man nonetheless persists in his prayer, striving to discern God even in the desert of loneliness by refusing to give in to this bleak distress—then can he be quite certain that he is really seeking God in his prayer; for no human being could lay upon us the compulsion so harsh and so lonely as is this effort, an effort which can be sustained only by the hope that at its end there is to be found God Himself.

So it is that time as well as manner is important in respect to prayer. How easily are we led astray by such a dictum as the one which tells us that *prayer is a necessity of a Christian life,* and how readily may we imagine that we have, with a few vocal prayers recited well or ill, fulfilled our obligation! An axiom of this kind is meaningful only in the event that certain conditions are fulfilled, as is also the case with that other axiom which tells us that *a ship must be in the water if it is to sail.* I may indeed throw a glass of water at the ship, but this will not be enough to raise it and set it under way. There must be a certain measure of water—a certain draught of water, as it is called. And so it is with the soul. In order that it be borne up and impelled toward God, the soul needs a certain measure of prayer, a certain draught of prayer. If that measure be deep and strong, so much more sure and swift will be the soul in its journey to God. On the other hand, prayer that is niggardly, prayer that is like a mere goblet of water, will leave the soul unmoved and quite lacking in capacity to move forward. It is by deep and urgent surgings that prayer lays hold upon the soul, to bear it, all at once and forever, out on to the high seas.

It is worth noting that in the first part of the Lord's Prayer nothing is said that has to do with anything but God: it deals with Him alone. The opening petitions of this prayer show in fact the best and most effective way of attaining to the presence of God.

Our Father. It is our conviction that we are sons of God that gives us the inclination and the courage to pray, and to present ourselves before God as children who hunger and who ask bread of their Father. Will He reward us with a serpent?

Who art in heaven. We are exhorted to seek God where He may be found; not among created things, nor in those objects which come naturally under our view, but above all that has been created. We can thus find God, all at once, in His own heavenly kingdom, through that detachment from created things which marks the effort to pray, as well as through the spiritual impulsion which it will arouse in us.

Hallowed be Thy name. It is by name that anyone is distinct from all others; the name is close to the heart, for it tells who one is: name and honor are inseparable. To pray that God's name may be accounted holy is, therefore, to desire that God may be known as He is; it is to wish to honor Him for His own sake; hence, actually to give Him the place which belongs to Him, by making room for Him completely. The name of God must be hallowed, that is to say, given a place on a level distinct and separate from every other name howsoever venerated; His is the only name at which every knee is to bow. Prayer offers this entire worship.

Thy kingdom come. The kingdom of God is, in the first place, God's complete and absolute dominion over the soul of man, who subjects himself freely to God with the consent of all his faculties in the supernatural obedience of faith and love. We pray that this kingdom may come, that God's sovereign lordship be universally recognized and be set above all other allegiances of mankind; we pray that this kingdom may subdue all other loyalties in a strong and gentle fashion, and that it may enrich them through the Cross. We pray especially that this kingdom may come within our own hearts and souls. We pray that, by the deep and personal meeting with Him which prayer achieves, God may take our hearts into His hands, making of them what He will. Then would our hearts be no longer capable of offending God: then would they truly be enclosed in the very heart of the kingdom, sustained and formed by the rulership of God over them, just as an infant is sustained and formed in the womb of its mother.

Thy will be done. It is by doing the will of God that we can best show that we love Him. He who loves God will do the will of God: it is thus that His kingdom will come. In these opening petitions of the Lord's Prayer there is nothing whatever said of us: all has to do with God; it is of *His* name, *His* kingdom, *His* will, that we think. Not even a glance is to be cast on anything at all but God. There is not even to be any explicit concern with our own salvation: here is really a case of that which comes by way of increase: "Make it your first care to find the Kingdom of God . . . and all these things shall be yours without the asking." There is not even any explicit mention of the most worthy of things, such as supernatural graces which we might ask *for ourselves*. If we strive in singleness of heart and with all our strength for the hallowing of God's name, for the realization of His sovereign dominion, for the fulfilment of His will, then surely all the rest—all other good things— will come to us, by way of increase; and by all the rest we understand especially our own eternal salvation and all needed graces in this life.

Let us then wish for the fulfilment of God's adorable will, such as it is in itself within the unsearchable depths of God's own heart, such as we can never really comprehend: for it is entirely beyond the capacities of all our foretelling and of the utmost stretches of our own wills. The will of God, just because it is the divine will, is far beyond us in every way. It would not indeed be divine were it not entirely beyond our understanding of it: then let us remain at peace, content in knowing that we are out of our depth and are in the hands of another. Let us have enough confidence in God to feel that this will, which is His own, is the very best that can be, just because it is His, and it can therefore intend only what is for our good, He being our Father, His good being our good. And, above all, let us never put our own narrow little wills in the place which belongs of right to the will of God. Let us bow to the will of God at once and without hesitation, accepting in it all that is unknown or seeming to involve risk. We will come to know it, little by little, as we grope our way, in proportion as we follow its strange unravellings. We may come to know it as the blind man does the threads in a net, grasping each mesh, but never seeing the whole. In thus doing God's will on earth, we cooperate in its fulfilment in heaven: we do not impede its accomplishment. We carry out on earth a will which is not earthly, a will which for that very reason often presents itself to us in so unexpected a guise. How often does it come like a beggar we meet on the way, one who though unknown to us asks of us that we give him all! For all the little attention that we may give him, scarcely opening our ears to his mysterious accents, how apt is he to leave us stripped of everything!

It is only after strongly setting forth what concerns God alone that we are told that we may ask something for ourselves or for our fellows. Thus is emphasis given to the lesson that understanding what prayer is: it demands that, for an instant at least, we put aside all else than God. If we would make use of set forms, we must not be enslaved by them, but use them only in order to transcend them and to cast ourselves beyond them into the deep places of God's own heart. And that is why it is well to make use, by preference, of simple words, especially of consecrated ones like the words of the Lord's Prayer, to use them deliberately and almost like incantations while our wills are bared before God, and we wish for nothing but for Him, for His kingdom, for His will, for the hallowing of His name. In the very beginning we are thus the master of our prayer; then

it is the prayer which takes hold of us and which carries us into the profound recesses wherein the soul
is united with God.

Even though we may pray for others, it is God
Himself who is first of all to be sought after: we pray
that His will may be wrought in all, for all, and by
all. To pray for anyone is *to love him in the presence
of God*. To love anyone is to wish him well and,
above all, to wish him well in whatever concerns the
best of all good things—his eternal salvation and his
participation in fulfilling the will of God. But the
important thing is to be already in God's presence
if we would love our fellows. To love others in a truly
Christian way, we must live always in God's presence;
we do good to them not in the measure in which we
are close to them but inasmuch as we are close to
God. For it is only in the measure that we are set
within the very heart of God that we will be able to
gain for those we love all the good that we wish for
them.

Besides, the second part of the Lord's Prayer never
sunders us from our fellowmen. What we ask is always in the plural, for *us;* it is without making dis-
tinctions between man and man that we pray. To begin with, we ask now for our daily bread. No doubt,
God wishes us to ask only for today's bread. We are
asked only to do what the children of this world do;
for they would never think of having yesterday's
bread for breakfast. This petition attains full meaning only if by it we mean by *daily bread* to ask in the
first place for the grace of God, and that Holy Spirit
would no more deny us than would we refuse bread

to our own hungry children. But in asking this love and this grace from God, we must ask only in the measure of the day's need; we must seek no more than grace for now, for the moment that *is*. All this is to be understood: that we are like children who ask for bread, that God gives to His children only the grace needed for the time being, that normally it does not even occur to children to ask for a week's food. It would seem to them absurd to do so. And surely none of us would rush to the baker's to buy a three weeks' supply of bread; for who does not know that such bread would soon be unfit to eat? Instead, we have enough confidence in the baker to believe that he will still be in business in three weeks' time. We ought to trust Providence at least as much. When we eat, we well know that it is only for the day; that tomorrow we will be hungry again; and that recurring hunger is a mark of health. We feel sure that the next day will bring its needed nourishment to satisfy our hunger. And little children, who are the hungriest of all, do not even give the matter a thought. Their parents are there to attend to it.

In the same way, we know very well that the grace that is given us today will just suffice to satisfy our need; that God will grant us just that amount of strength which will enable us to hold on for the time being. Yet, that is enough; tomorrow we will again be given what grace we require, strength enough for the day's work. Living with God, we will always find the table well laid. If only we pray, we can be certain of lacking for nothing so long as we remain with Him. How rude it would be were we to ask our host for some guarantee about all the meals to be served while we visited him! In life and in death we are the guests of the loving God; and the worst thing that can be said about us is that we so often behave in His house like spoiled children. Such children He does not like.

"There was a man that gave a great supper, and sent out many invitations. And when the time came for his supper, he sent one of his own servants telling the invited guests to come, for all was now ready. And all of them, with one accord, began making excuses. I have bought a farm, the first said to him, and I must needs go and look over it; I pray thee, count me excused. And another said, I have bought five pair of oxen, and I am on my way to make trial of them; I pray thee, count me excused. And another said, I have married a wife, and so I am unable to come. The servant came back and told his master all this, whereupon the host fell into a rage, and said to his servant, Quick, go out into the streets and lanes of the city; bring in the poor, the cripples, the blind and the lame. . . . I tell you, none of those who were first invited shall taste of my supper."

This banquet is communion with God in prayer. There is no one who may excuse himself from taking part. There is no valid excuse which will dispense man from prayer. Yet all the reasons advanced by these guests were good; there was no evil in what they had done. It is a good act to have bought a field and then to wish to survey it; to try the oxen, to set out upon a wedding journey. Nevertheless, the host was angered that all these men stayed away from the banquet. For prayer is not one duty among many another. It does not prevent us from tilling our fields, from working our oxen, from joining in marriage; but we must know that we have to withdraw, from time to time, from even the most legitimate occupations in order to make a place in our lives for God.

Nothing then can dispense us from our obligation to pray, for prayer is the practice of the love of God. Regardless of our poverty, our blindness, our limping, or whatever else it may be that troubles us, we must pray. Let us come before God just as we are, with empty hands, as poor men, as beggars. Let us approach Him, even though we must drag ourselves haltingly along as those who are blind. Even stumbling and limping, let us come before Him, even if we must walk like cripples. But let us take our first step. Let us begin the journey to meet Him. And let us never stop until we have found Him.

I WILL DWELL WITH THEM

Is THERE really a place where we may find God and live with Him?

It is true, of course, that He is everywhere by reason of His creative action. All things receive from Him their being and their continuance in that being. Were God to close His eyes all the world would vanish. His is a sovereign presence; His a lordship which embraces all things without any favoritism or any cessation, an entire dominion over every one and every thing, even over the demons, a power which girds itself about whatever exists to the extent of being the reason for all that exists. Yet, this very immensity, by which God is revealed in all creation, hides Him from us. And this omnipresence, whereby He ceaselessly surrounds us, is the reason that He escapes our notice. God is everywhere. Yet in all things we behold only His external aspect; and we but dimly understand how in them we may worship the almighty Lord who dwells in light inaccessible. We cast ourselves down before His actual divine perfections; but the very divinity of His attributes shrouds them in a veil of mystery.

Are we then to rise no higher than those who, without hope, lift their hands to a brazen sky, crying aloud to one who will never answer? Are we to raise, on our high hills, an altar to the Unknown God? "I tell you," said St. Paul to the men of Athens, "God . . . is not far from any one of us; it is in Him that we live, and move, and have our being. Thus, some of your own poets have told us, for indeed we are His children."

We are, in fact, immersed in God. If we wish to know His adorable face better than we do, we have only to look into the mirror of our own nature. We resemble God, as a child does his parent: we are of His family. Man carries throughout the universe the illusive image of the being at whose feet the whole of creation lies. "And God said: Let us make man wearing Our own image and likeness: let us put him in command of . . . the whole earth." God is thus to be discerned in all material things upon which He has left traces of Himself. But when this likeness rises to the higher aspects of relationship, may it not be discerned in another and even more perfect manner in a creature with whom He was especially pleased? God is a spirit. If, then, we are in His image, it is in the spirit that we must be like Him. God being the Word and Love, man is like Him in the sense that he also possesses an intelligence for the perception of the truth, and a will which embodies the spiritual force of this enlightened intellect. The intellectual nature of man is a particular figure of the Trinity.

But is it possible for us to come nearer to God than simile and image allow us? It was of a closer kind of relationship that Jesus spoke, on that night of Holy

Thursday when the stars shone in the sky like the lamps of love in the great Song of Songs. For Jesus said: "If a man has any love for Me, he will be true to My word: and then he will win My Father's love and we will both come to him and make Our continual abode with him." The place in which God dwells is within ourselves. Such is the universal law of Christianity: it is a likeness which expands into a real indwelling of the Divine within us.

We can, without becoming paradoxical, say that the initial stirring of the presence of God within us is in the realization of His absence. It was observed by a naturalist scholar that "man is a religious animal." This proposition is well put, and it amounts to saying: the natural exactions of our nature make us tend toward God.

It is, however, by a negative and indirect manner of expression that we conceive of God as being different from all that surrounds us, and as the necessary complement of an imperfect world, strangely like the essentially hypothetical and despaired-of fulfilment of our own nature. Why should it be surprising that the image leads to its archetype? I would simply observe here that our will to see God, our capacity for participating in the divine life, already indicate an *absence* of Him and of that divine life He bestows in us. But the very fact of absence suggests the possibility of presence: the empty chair allows us to await the coming of that mysterious Companion who, even now perhaps, is about to seat Himself beside us, as did once He who walked upon the way to the inn at Emmaüs. "See where I stand at the door, knocking;

if anyone listens to My voice and opens the door, I
will come in to visit him, and take My supper with
him, and he shall sup with Me." At the eternal supper of the Lord we are called to rejoice in the presence of God who, now in the secret communion of
prayer, as later in the full light of the vision of Him
face to face, will feed us of His own substance.

There is no earthly food but leaves us forever un-
satisfied. Whether we like it or not, ever since God
has willed to come to meet us, the very issue of our
final destiny drives us into His presence: we will find
Him at last as our judge, if we have refused to know
Him as our friend. Besides He does not force Himself upon us by fear, and He will not be loved unless
it be by love freely given. But for all that, unbelievers ought concern themselves with Him: their very
doubt should drive them to pray. May their hearts
be opened to the unknown! May they cry out and
beg God to manifest Himself to them! Even should
there be no God, what have they to lose? In the everlasting night of their solitude, they would hear no
reply. And yet: "Ask, and the gift will come; seek
and you shall find; knock and the door shall be
opened to you. Everyone that asks, will receive; that
seeks, will find; that knocks, will have the door
opened to him."

No one calls upon God in vain. A wordless voice,
a voice unheard before—or perhaps one recognized
and familiar as friendship—speaks gently and makes
itself heard within the soul: "Fear not, it is I. I am
your God. Long have I been your comfort and your
help. I am with you; even though you have known

it not, the right hand of My justice has sustained you. Do not draw back from this Hand wounded for love of you—I am the Lord, your God. I have redeemed you. I have called you by your name. You are Mine." It is in one blinding flash that God makes Himself known to be God, and God known to the soul: "All through the night my soul has yearned for thee," as the Prophet has said, "to thee my heart aspires, watching for the dawn. . . . The dew Thou sendest, Lord, shall bring light. The night of my doubt and my longing is enlightened by hope." *Ex dixi: forsitan tenebrae conculcabunt me, et nox illuminatio mea in deliciis meis* (And I said: Perhaps darkness shall cover me, and night shall be my light in my pleasures).

There is a very common misunderstanding today. It being granted that God is infinitely good, it appears to some that we are justified in loving whatever we like, and that—so long as we are not given to hatred or blasphemy—all the pleasures of life are compatible with the service of One who is, by essence, Love. We are at the point of being overwhelmed by mystics who wish to lead our souls over all the paths of the earth whereon our hearts may go astray. There is a mysticism of race, of nationalism, of class; a mysticism of art, and of adventure, of opium, and of other drugs—all types of mysticism which lend to the weaknesses of our flesh the tinsel glow of a spurious divinity.

Now God is never in any sense to be coupled with anything other than Himself. He is a refining fire, devouring all beside Himself. His dwelling place is beyond the reach of flesh and blood. It is by an un-allowable kind of presumption that any creature would seek to love God in himself. To see or to love God, one must already be with God, either by nature or in virtue of a real kind of adoptive sonship which has marked our souls with a capacity to participate in His divinity. This sharing in the divine nature is something more precious than the whole universe: it is the grace God freely gives us. "I am the Lord thy God . . . thy deliverer. . . . So prized, so honored, so dearly loved, that I am ready to give up mankind in thy place, a world to save thee. Do not be afraid, I am with thee." In the divine scale of values it is God alone who counts. If we appear to have value in His eyes, it is because we are His. It is for this reason that by grace we are newly born and brought forth into a life that is wholly new. "Believe Me when I tell thee this," Jesus declared to Nicodemus, "a man cannot see the kingdom of God without being born anew. . . . What is born by natural birth is a thing of nature, and what is born by spiritual birth is a thing of spirit. . . . No man has ever gone up into heaven but there is one who has come down from heaven. . . ." The father of Origen bent over his newly baptized son and venerated in him the temple of the living God. Truly and even without knowing it, such a child already sleeps in paradise in the state of grace. He is carried in the very heart of God, is cradled within His paternal arms. Yet it is only by awakening to knowledge of himself that he becomes capable of loving this embrace. The Queen of Sheba came from the ends of the earth to marvel

at the splendor of Solomon, and truly here is one
greater than Solomon.

Man, poor as he is, all at once is clothed by the
Spirit, and is enclosed in a mysterious process of re-
birth which forms him anew, heals him, totally
restores him, and makes a mystic life fluid to flow
within him. In miraculous strength, eternity itself is
poured into the soul of man, leading him into wide
places hitherto unknown. The kingdom of God is
truly like the leaven which the busy housewife put
into the three measures of wheat that the whole
might rise. Divine grace is a leaven which fills all the
substance of man and raises him up; penetrates
deeply into his faculties, bringing them to fruition,
and lifting them into a supernatural life which is the
very life of God. For in the three measures men-
tioned in the parable the Fathers of the Church have
always seen the human soul, a figure in this life of the
Blessed Trinity.

A figure it is indeed; but an image much darkened
—even disfigured—by the stain of sin. It is a living
mirror, but one shrouded by the darkness of ignor-
ance. May there dawn upon it the eternal morning in
which the Sun of Justice shall shine forth! To reflect
the brilliance of that Sun's splendor, the disfigured
mirror—which is created man—must purify itself of
every earthly taint. "It must needs be," says Ruysbroeck, "that the spirit of man become ever like unto
God, by returning to the path of grace and the virtues, wherefrom it had fallen by the fact of mortal
sin. For if man be made according to the likeness of
God, that is to say that he has been made apt for

grace; and grace is that divine light which, by the intense penetration of its rays, makes us like God. Unless this light bathe us in that holy likeness, we are unable to unite ourselves supernaturally to God. Despite the likeness which is in us, and the naturally inalienable unity which we share with God, if we lose the divine likeness which is given us by grace, we shall indeed be lost forever. Therefore, from the time that God perceives in us a readiness to receive this grace, His free bounty to us inclines Him to renew our life by making us like Himself. . . . He impresses upon us His image and likeness, in an outpouring of His gifts and of His very self. He frees us from our sins, ransoming us, and making us like Himself. Then under the very same divine action which blots out our sins and gives us likeness to divinity and liberty in love, the spirit of man is adorned with the love which begets its own increase. Then does the soul step forth, supernaturally and without any intermediary, to that great confrontation and union in which is found man's highest degree of heavenly happiness."

In the whole universe, the spirit occupies a special place in the scale of things. It has the capacity, while remaining substantially the same, of becoming something else; of taking on the appearance of an object external to itself; of living—on another plane than that of its own physical existence—the life of another than itself, which life it is able to experience in addition to its own. It can even take on the outward semblance of a nature different from itself without, however, extinguishing the distinction which divides the two. The spirit becomes other insofar as that other has otherness. All is grist to its mill. In its transparency it has the capacity to reflect all things with so high a degree of intensity that its special and inherent quality as a spirit is to become absolutely identified with the object it knows, just as though it had swallowed it up in itself. This assimilatory power is actually a true presence of the object known in the center of the knowing mind or spirit. We commonly say of something which we have comprehended or understood—and *comprehendere* means to take with us, or rather unto us—"I have completely absorbed this thing into my being; it has become part of me." There is no longer a question of two essentially different things lying side by side or being juxtaposed; but rather there has occurred a mutual and fully shared penetration in that kind of functioning which belongs, of its very nature, to the spirit. It is an intimate degree of fusion, a kind of mingling of the spirit known and loved with the spirit of the knower and lover. The real characteristic of the spirit being its power to depart from itself in order to enter into something other than itself—the ability to project its own life into another being in which it will itself come to flowering and of which it will employ the dynamic force and natural gifts— the spirit therefore attains a particular kind of unity with its object, a unity of its very nature spiritual and even more wonderful than the union of soul and body; that is to say, it attains to an absoluteness of identity in the order of what is intended.

But here the special note of the case lies in the

fact that God, the *object of knowledge* (or thing known), is at once the first cause and the ontological root of *the knowing subject* (or the knower). As such, He already exists in the soul by reason of His being present to all creation—by his immensity, as it is called, both creative and conserving. However, this divine attribute attaches us to God in a manner which, if even more intimate than the way in which we are attached to ourselves, is nevertheless only a manner external to Himself: it makes us gravitate toward Him as the universal center of attraction. All that we have and are is primarily from God: in respect to us, God's immensity is nothing more than the creaturely relationship of servitude, in which we naturally stand toward Him, and that right of divine dominion over all that we are and have. Yet, however deep may be our understanding of this philosophical truth, it advances us no whit further in learning the secrets of divine life.

But it is Jesus who has said: "I do not speak of you any more as My servants; a servant is one who does not understand what his master is about, whereas I have made known to you all that My Father has told Me; and so I have called you My *friends.*"

Nevertheless, even grace—if it be considered as something created and unperfected—grants to us no more intimate presence of God than is the effect of His immensity. However, if it be considered according to its essential tendency and its unfailing force, grace shatters with heavenly impetuosity the brazen gates and it unlocks the bolts which guard God's secrets. Just because it is ordained and directed by

God, grace flows joyously toward God, carrying us into the very heart of the Trinity. And it is in this impulsion that its most characteristic work consists, that it brings us to God Himself in that friendship by which the soul knows God intimately as He dwells in it; by that capacity to enter into God Himself, a capacity which rewards us with the gift of the Three Divine Persons to be our own, to such an extent that we act in union with Them, ourselves sharing in Their life. Their life is our life. Our conversation is with the Trinity as on high. Our human heart becomes a fountain of love springing up in the heart of God. "On the last and greatest day of the feast Jesus stood there and cried aloud, If any man is thirsty, let him come to Me, and drink; yes, if a man believe in Me, as the Scripture says, Fountains of living water shall flow from his bosom." To which St. John gives us the gloss that "He was speaking here of the Spirit, which was to be received by those who had learned to believe in Him."

All at once, and throughout our entire being, God touches us in a determining contact by which we are, as it were, used up: God alone, in His glory, remains within us. From the time of the infusion of His grace, God has opened Himself to us that we may entrust ourselves to Him. The enlightened soul distinguishes with wonderment the sources and springs of the life of Him from whom he draws all, recognizing His presence as he had not done before. The very God who, hitherto, had appeared as mighty and afar off, is now offering to the soul not alone His own existence and active powers, but Himself as the principle and motive of its activity, as its bread of life above the life of nature, so that it may be united with God and made to partake of His divine nature. This is, indeed, a knowing of God, and is consequently a real contact with Him resulting in a penetration in the order of intent; but here the divinity is known less as a separate entity than as present in the soul of man, newly present as a lover in the very center of the human heart sustained in life by God. For in order that one may make use of something, it is necessary first to be in possession of it.

This knowledge of God's nearness, of His presence within us, a presence by which through grace we do His work, is really a new mode of the divine presence, one engrafted upon that presence proper to the immensity of God. Suddenly, there is revealed to our eyes the hidden yet ever-present Godhead. We are now able to think of Him, to enjoy Him to a certain extent, to learn—almost by touching—the outlines of His living reality; and He Himself imparts to us the gift of His creative eye. God, we are accustomed to say, is almighty, afar off; He dwells above the skies, in the heaven of heavens; but this is not the case: God is here, within us! His mightiness is a *being present* to us, which enlivens us. His apparent far-offness from us represents the high nature of His rulership of our lives. And His tremendous elevation is the great depth of His love. God sits at the very center of our souls, offering Himself to the love of the believer. In truth, our soul is an awesome thing. It is verily the house of God and the gate of heaven. Assuredly, it is here that the Lord dwells: He has poured out his glory upon us and we have known it not.

What hitherto unperceived meaning is now to be discerned in the promises of Isaias, "I will give to you hidden treasures and the key to secrets which are locked up, so that you may know that I am the Lord who has called you by your name"! And how there shines forth a resplendent certainty of meaning in the words, *Assimilavi te!*—I will gather you up, I will take you up unto myself. You shall live My life, I being the soul of your soul; I have made you to be reborn in Me; you are Mine and come from Me as a child that has been carried in its mother's womb. "And he who sat on the throne said, Behold I make all things new. These words I was bidden write down, words most sure and true. And He said to me, It is over. I am Alpha and Omega, the beginning of all things and their end; those who are thirsty shall drink—it is My free gift—out of the spring whose water is life. Who wins the victory? He shall have his share in this."

"Who wins the victory? He shall have his share in this." It is under this kind of enlightenment that one must take account of the exactions required by prayer, as well as the patience of the saints. Whatever they may be, the troubles of this life do not weigh at all in comparison with the glory that is to be, the glory that shall be shown forth in us. This thought should go far to sustain us here below in that spiritual combat which is more bloody than any human battle. This kingdom of God within us is for the violent. One may always come closer to God "by steps of love," ever entering more fully into the secrets of His light, and losing oneself in it as grasshoppers do in the sun. *Dominus vobiscum.* God is reborn in us by the strength of His own life. Just as was the word of the angel to the Blessed Virgin, so also is the word of the priest—*Dominus vobiscum*—at once an announcement and an invitation, an assurance of a presence which is real although mystical. As at Nazareth, it is again the promise of a birth miraculous and beyond our power to describe. The mystical body of Christ is also conceived by a *Fiat* of love—*Let it be done unto me according to His Word*—and the strength of the Holy Spirit overshadows the soul. "You are the temple of the living God; God has told you so; I will live and move among them, and be their God, and they shall be My people. . . ." And therefore, as the Apostle remarks, since we have such a promise, let us cleanse ourselves of every blemish of flesh or spirit, working out our salvation in the fear of God.

God fulfils His promise by paying unceasing visits to the pure soul. He renews in it the coming to pass of His eternal fruitfulness and the enrichment which His infinite love arouses. His divine generative power, which has its eternal end or object in the Person of the Word, has also an object in the order of time, as there is fulfilled by grace the mission of that same Word in the soul of man. The procession—or sharing in mutual love of Father and Son—which generates the Holy Ghost in His everlasting personality has likewise an object or term in time: the sanctification of souls. Thus may a human soul in the state

of grace know God by His Word, and love Him by
His Holy Spirit. Every time is God so reborn anew
in the soul of man; and the fruit of this birth is the
overflowing of the Holy Spirit with all His gifts. The
soul is plunged into—indeed, it is submerged by—
the deep waters of the divine life. It slips beyond its
own limitations in the exercise of a wisdom and a
love greater than any which earth knows: the soul is
become the dwelling of God, impelled and inspired
by Him, delighting in Him, and being nourished by
His very life. In this close union with God, and made
a part of those mysterious exchanges of divine life
communicated between the Three Divine Persons,
the soul experiences a close union with the Incarnate
Word and knows dimly—but with certainty—that it
is become the well-beloved child of the Father, the
temple of the Holy Spirit. It is this wonderful filial
relationship, this mysterious blending of two into
one, this entire giving of the self to the Holy Spirit,
which raises the Christian to the dizzying height of
the Holy Trinity.

Now, all such wonders are wholly unperceived by
the natural senses. They exist only in the life of faith.
They can be present in the heart alongside of desola-
tion and anguish. And what need would I have of a
God of my own dimensions, or of a God at my own
level and as weak as myself? God is Pure Light; and
it is precisely because of this that He affects our eyes,
as the sun does the owl. "What we make known is
the wisdom of God, His secret, kept hidden till now;
so, before the ages, God has decreed, reserving glory
for us. None of the rulers of this world could read

His secret. . . . Things no eye has seen, no ear has heard, no human heart conceived, the welcome God has prepared for those who love Him. To us, then, God has made a revelation of it through His Spirit; there is no depth in God's nature so deep that the Spirit cannot find it out. Who else can know a man's thoughts, except the man's own spirit that is within him? So no one else can know God's thoughts, but the Spirit of God. And what we have received is no spirit of worldly wisdom; it is the Spirit that comes from God, to make us understand God's gifts to us. . . ."

Such knowledge as we have, being dim and partial, is of course no more than a slight and provisional supplement to that wholly spiritual food whereby the angels are filled, and for which we hunger. The human soul suffers great pains in the love which increases its hunger, while giving it at the same time a more definite and tantalizing foretaste of the table which is spread in heaven. Solace, peace, joy, fulfilment of gifts, beauty, all that makes for happiness— these are found in God, and found beyond any measuring, as He appears to the enlightened eye of the believer. This desire for God is enough to cause one to wish for death, as the price of seeing Him. Indeed Bossuet remarked that "the man who does not wish for death is no Christian."

One would have to be able to give measurement to God in order to estimate the degree of perfection in a soul which would know how to make itself ready to dwell on so high a level. It is worth while, therefore, to seek here the testimony of those who have undergone this kind of spiritual experience. "The soul," says Ruysbroeck, "is abandoned to itself as though without being, and is plunged into that darkness in which contemplative souls are engulfed, incapable of ever again re-establishing themselves in the state of being proper to creatures. In the great depth of this darkness the loving soul dies to itself by beginning to know God and the life which is for all eternity. . . . *All of the gifts which are in God by His nature become our possessions in Him through love,* and they are of God in us by the means of that great love which is His Holy Spirit: it is in that love that one may taste all one has desired."

Just as God is neither wisdom, nor truth, nor goodness, nor this, nor that, but embodies absolutely all perfection in His most high and sovereign simplicity, so the saint is neither magnanimous, nor humble, nor sweet, nor strong, nor just, nor merciful: he is all of these; but in a fashion wholly his own, in a fashion infinitely free, unforeseen, and paradoxical. Every Christian virtue exercises itself in his heart upon a foundation exquisitely lovable. This is what little Thérèse of the Child Jesus teaches us in saying: "In the heart of my Mother, the Church, I will be love, and thus I will be all."

What one may sense is that such a soul, taken up from the world and raised to ecstatic heights in the very heart of the Trinity, is possessed by God to such a degree as to be oblivious of all else and of very self. One of this sort is even more withdrawn from mortal affairs than one who is physically dead, and is actually no more than a cadaver glowing with a great flame. The impetuous flow of grace in such a soul would seem to lend to it a capricious impulsiveness were it not under the most unrestrained obedience to the Spirit, and thus raised beyond mortal judgment. To Ezechiel was given a frightening vision of four living creatures: "Each of them marched straight forward, following the movement of a divine impulse, never swerving as he marched. There was that, too, in the appearance of the living figures which put me in mind of flaming coals, or of torches; that was what I saw going to and fro in the midst of the living figures, a glow as of fire, and from this glow lightning came out. So the living creatures came and went, vivid as lightning-flashes."

It is not without point to observe here that this teaching is the very opposite of pantheism. God is not fashioned by the soul wherein He dwells. Neither does He come about as the result of a naturally religious disposition in man. Notwithstanding how high may be any man's degree of personal refinement, of intelligence, or of understanding, no matter what may be his gifts of heart or of temperament, however generously noble may be his nature—not one of these qualities gives him any right to enjoy the presence or the friendship of God; nor do they of themselves lead him into it. It is God who first inclines Himself to the soul, who first opens the way that leads to Himself by granting the soul His pardon and His grace. In every case, it is God who has been the first to open His heart to man. At all times, the presence of God within the soul keeps its character of a confrontation which, on the part of God, is voluntary and gratuitous.

Without any injustice to us, God could enclose Himself wholly in His own happiness; and it is with some degree of terror that one beholds Him condescending with so much love to our wretchedness. There is no question, either, of the absorption of two beings into one. In heaven, the beatified intelligence is immediately fulfilled in the Word, and the Holy Spirit will be the accomplishment of our eternal happiness. Nevertheless, the substance of the Deity remains infinitely distinct and quite separate from the substance of each created being: it and they are entitatively untouched. The divine substance will be revealed to the blessed without itself being subjected to any change. This is not difficult to understand, and may be illustrated even from the order of things perceptible to the senses, as in the case of a tree which is seen by the beholder. This act of seeing changes nothing of the tree, yet nevertheless it is really true that the one who sees beholds an object which before being seen was not perceptible to his sight. The blessed in heaven behold God as He is; and this vision transforms them without causing them to lose their own nature: on the contrary, it marvelously completes and complements that nature. Yet God remains as He was and is; and so He will remain forever and ever. He becomes the joy of His chosen ones, without Himself suffering the slightest loss or increase of His own infinite beatitude. Such is the radiant and unchanging Trinity—a boundless ocean of peace, of light, and of happiness.

We will know God fully, as He knows Himself. We will have become like Him. Just as in all the simplicity of His power He is at once the knower and the known, so will He be both the object of our seeing and the light by which we see. He will be, moreover, the total cause—deeply rooted in our being—of our intellectual nature and of its functioning. The image will have flowered into reality. God will be all in all. The blessed country will be full of the knowledge of the Lord just "as the waters cover the sea." Then will the Church complete her unity, "two natures in one spirit," and like Esther the Queen, having passed through each door, will finally gaze upon the King in all His beauty.

"Esther . . . put on all her fine array, queenly robes that dazzled the eye . . . then bade two of her waiting-maids bear her company. On one she leant, as though her dainty form must needs be supported; the other followed her mistress as train-bearer. Alluring beauty of flushed cheek and shining eye hid a heart grief-stricken, a heart ready to swoon with fear. Door after door she passed, till she reached the king's presence, where he sat on his royal throne, royally clad, amid a glitter of gold and jewels; terrible of mien. No sooner had he looked up . . . than the queen was ready to swoon away; white went her cheeks as she leaned her head, fainting, on the maid that stood by. And now the king . . . started from his throne in trembling haste, and was fain to hold her in his arms till she came to herself; and still with soothing words he reassured her: Esther, what is amiss with thee . . . ? Were I thy own brother, thou hast not less cause to fear. . . . Thou hast but to come near, and touch my scepter. And with that, for she was voiceless still, he raised his golden scepter and touched her neck with it; then kissed her and asked, What, hast thou no word for me? My lord, she said, the sight of thee overawed me, as if I had seen one of God's angels; sweet reverence does thy majesty inspire. For indeed, my lord, there is nothing about thee but must be admired, nothing in thy looks but is gracious."

I CAME TO BEAR WITNESS
TO THE TRUTH

As ONE BENDS over a crib, gazing at a new-born baby, one sees a little body sensitive to cold, and easily bruised, a body which stirs awkwardly but yet conceals an immortal soul still drowsily unaware of its surroundings. How quickly are we apt to think to ourselves: What will this child become? What destiny awaits him? What is to be his mission in this world?

So it is that on Christmas Day there is sung in our churches an anthem which draws Christian people to the crib in a stable where there sleeps upon a bed of straw, between an ox and an ass, a newly born Child: *Puer natus est nobis,* "Unto us a child is born." A child is born for our sake. Now, therefore, this midnight birth of an Infant God gives rise to a quite different question from that we think of in connection with the birth of other children. In times of discouragement, at an evil suggestion of the Great Enemy, a cry often comes from the depths of our abandoned souls: "After all, it was not I who asked to be given birth and life." Well then, let us look at the little Jesus in His crib of straw: He is in the midst of us as one of us, capable of suffering, of anguish, of tears, even of death; but, nevertheless, He

asked that He might be born and live. As God He
lacked for nothing, He did not have to come. He was
under no necessity to become less happy; He need
never have been born into this vale of tears; He
nevertheless chose so to be, and He selected the time
of His coming, choosing also the place, His race, and
His mother. The question which thought of this
Child brings to our mind is not *What will He become?* but, *Inasmuch as He has chosen to be born
among us, why did He do it?*

And Jesus Himself gives answer to this question.
In order to lend to that answer a most solemn note,
He chose the very moment of His condemnation to
death by Pilate to explain officially His birth and
His coming into the world: "What I was born for,
what I came into the world for, is to bear witness to
the truth." From the time He was born of a young
girl of immaculate purity, this little Child was a witness: while yet in her arms His role—unique among
all the children of men—was none other than to bear
witness to the truth.

Now, just what is a witness? A witness is someone
perfectly informed of something unknown to others,
who reveals this hidden knowledge and proves it by
the authority with which He speaks. Nothing could
be more correctly stated than to say of the Child
Jesus that He is a witness, and that the object of His
birth in time was to provide a means for Him to
bear this witness. The hidden truth—to knowledge of
which we could not naturally come—the hidden
truth of which He was born to be the witness, is God
Himself, Truth subsisting in the fullness of His di-

vine nature, the inexpressible union of Father, Son, and Holy Spirit, equal in power and majesty, in one divine substance, revealing Themselves to us by faith, giving Themselves to us in love, and drawing us to eternal association with Them in heavenly happiness; this hidden truth is God with us, God for us, in that supreme cleaving of all that we are to all that God is.

Three qualities are required of a witness. First of all, he must have knowledge of that about which he speaks. Who is there who is able to bear witness concerning God? Is not God hidden in light inaccessible? Who can penetrate the inviolable secret of that Unknown God of whom St. John says that "no man has ever seen Him"? But he immediately adds: "Now His only-begotten Son . . . has Himself brought us a clear message." It is God alone who can know and speak of God. And this little Child is God. He is the substantial self-revelation of God, the King of angels who by His wondrous works will bring into subjection to Himself heaven, earth, and hell; He it is who will forgive the sins of men and who, of His own power, will arise from the tomb. This little Child, sleeping now in the manger, is not simply God's messenger, His representative, or His prophet: He is God's Son. Nor is His sonship in any manner inferior or adoptive: He is the Son of God by nature, equal to the Father, and is Himself really and substantially God to the extent that beside Him there is no other God; He is God in the fullness and in the complete expression of His glory.

Neither all the angels of heaven nor all the wise men of the earth are enough to convince me that this

Child is God: I would not, indeed, believe a truth of this kind on the testimony of all the angels or of all the philosophers; it is the Child Himself who reaches my heart and implants in it the conviction of the truthfulness and of the love of my God. He Himself is the proof of that which He came to witness; He Himself is the affirmation unsurpassed of the love of God; He is the gift of God and His revelation. In Jesus is the manifestation of God, His epiphany; He is God who loves us and who shows Himself to us; He is God become our own. This Child is more than the tremendous and abstract *I am* of the religious philosopher. He is more than the stern lawgiver of the old Jews who wrote His commandments upon tablets of stone, and who breaks the necks of the rebellious under His inflexible yoke. Our Christian God is a God made man, purely born of a pure virgin; He strikes terror into the hearts of the evil, but He is full of merciful help for repentant sinners; He is a God very close to man through His sacraments, especially so by the Eucharist; a God who brought to the apex of fulfilment His witness to the divine truth He Himself is when He shed the last drop of His blood upon the Cross.

A further quality exacted of a witness is that he can be understood. To what end will all my knowledge of an event serve you if I cannot speak to you in your own language? Hitherto God had chosen intermediaries to speak to men. The Jews, indeed, said to Moses: "Do thou tell us the message. . . . Do not let us hear the Lord speaking; it will cost us our lives." In order to know God well the knower must

Himself be God; but to speak clearly to men, the speaker must be one among them. And it is this which has now happened: God is made man that He may be more easily grasped and understood by men. This little Child brings God most fully to us while, under the veil of infirmity, He hides the tremendous glory of His majesty. God has taken human flesh, an entire human nature, body and soul, a real body of flesh and bone which is neither a mere appearance nor a phantom; He is a free and thinking soul, as is each of us. This Child is indeed of our race and family; He has proven it by His birth from a woman, virgin though she is; He will further prove it by His sufferings and death, undergone for us that we may know Him to be God, that we may know how great is His love of us. *It is I, the Cause of all things, who now speak to you.* Yes; this little Child is born just to tell us of God; and in Him it is God who shows Himself to us in such manner that we are really able to see Him. In this Child, filled with grace and truth, we see our own wretched human nature elevated to be a witness giving testimony to God, faithful testimony having its term in the very presence among us of that divinity to which the Child bears witness, while He, Himself Divine Truth, sleeps in the arms of the Virgin Mary.

But what lends authority to any witness is the dignity, the trustworthiness, which inhere in him personally: it is really these which establish the truth of his testimony, which aid the hearer to relate what he has been told to what objectively exists. Now, ought we attach very much importance to this Child's testimony? There is not a tribunal in the world, after all, before which the authority of a child's testimony amounts to very much. Yet, the personality of this Child is in no way veiled, as is that of other children, in that dark lack of understanding which is the mark of inexperience: He is already perfectly informed of all that is most worthy and most elevated; because of His divinity He is of infinite eminence; and not to give weight to His testimony is to blaspheme. *Jesus is Himself God.* Any man who wishes his testimony to be taken seriously will give it on his word of honor, and in the eyes of honorable men that word suffices to bind him to it. In order to corroborate His testimony God has given us His own Word; and it is inconceivable that He could be further bound; for this *Word* is Himself divine. The Word of God is the true Son of God; and it is this eternal Word who, in the complete simplicity of His person, possesses at the same time both human nature and divine nature: He effects a substantial union of these two natures, a union in which they suffer neither lessening nor confusion but are each fulfilled to perfection.

The very heart of the mystery of Christ lies in this basic unity, despite the inexpressible difference in these two natures. This unity is rooted wholly in the perfection of the divine *I am,* who is able to appropriate to Himself a created nature and actually to exercise every potentiality which belongs to it. This little Child who laughs and cries like all the other sons of men, who is nourished by the milk of a young Mother, herself pure to a degree beyond our power to express, this little Child is the Word of God enclosed in human flesh. He is God manifesting and expressing Himself by the substantial gift of Himself to us. Now have we no longer any need of Moses, nor of the stone tables of the Old Covenant. How can we now fail to understand, for evermore, the language in which the God-Man speaks to us?

Christianity does not embody, on the one hand, Christ born at Bethlehem two thousand years ago, crucified at Jerusalem, risen from the dead, and gone up into heaven; and, on the other hand, Christians going to Mass on Sundays and supporting the activities of the Church. No, it is wholly upon Jesus that Christianity is built; it is completely and entirely summed up in the little Child whom the Virgin Mary holds out to us. No one can become a Christian, no one is a Christian, save in the measure in which he conforms himself by a mystical, but nonetheless real, incorporation into the one life that is all-sufficing, the life of Jesus. For some grave reason one may be dispensed from going to Mass on Sunday, or from abstinence from meat on Friday; but the highest authority in the Church could never dispense a Christian from his need to believe in Jesus, to hope in Jesus, to unite his own heart to the Sacred Heart of Jesus, King and Center of all hearts. Even though we have not asked to be born, we know the end to which our lives and our deaths alike are pointing. May we be forever delivered by the Child Jesus from all foolish thoughts of despair: may He who willed to be born to live and to die bearing witness to divine truth incarnate in Himself, may He teach us that it is our mission to bear the same witness, even to the point of martyrdoms! Our lives and our deaths are in our hands in the sense that we can spend them uselessly and aimlessly if we will; but what end will be served if we gain the whole world and yet have never known, loved, or deserved God in Jesus? Life and death have been given us so that we may conform ourselves to that great mystery which lies at the very heart of Christianity—the life and death of the Lord Jesus.

Under the auspices of the American Dominicans there exists an association—the Holy Name Society— which numbers within its ranks hundreds of thousands of men who are bound by but one obligation, that on every occasion which presents itself they publicly profess their belief in the divinity of Jesus Christ. The assumption of such an obligation, provided it be loyally adhered to, can give meaning to an entire lifetime. A great light has shone in the night for those who are of right heart. Let us live and die in the light of this testimony: the very brightness of the Godhead shining forth resplendently from the adorable face of Jesus.

Sᴛ. Jᴏʜɴ, in speaking of Christ, recounts to us these words of Caiphas: "It is best for us if one man is put to death for the sake of the people, to save a whole nation from destruction." The evangelist notes that Caiphas spoke in his official capacity as high priest of that year, thus *prophesying* that the death of Jesus would be for the nation's sake, for Israel; and not indeed for Israel alone, but in order that all the children of God who were dispersed might be reassembled in unity.

This prophetic spirit of the ancient priesthood and its rites culminated in the bloody altar of the Cross and then re-established itself in the eternal priesthood and liturgy of the New Covenant, where there is celebrated the unfailing memorial of the sacrifice of Jesus, a true and real re-enactment of the sorrowful memory which it evokes and preserves. *O memoriale mortis Domini!* O remembrance of the Lord's death!

And it is, moreover, in such a sense that we are to take the words of Jesus when He instituted the Holy Eucharist: "This is My Blood, of the New Testament. . . . Do this for a commemoration of Me."

From the evening of Maundy Thursday, the sacraments of the Ancient Law became, as it were, extinct: their symbolism found its fulfilment and consummation in the tremendous fact of the death of the Man-God. In its sacramental truth, this death was already accomplished by the holy and venerable hands of Jesus, under the appearances of bread and wine, at the Last Supper. The fonts of life which, on the morrow, would flow from the five wounds, the Body bleeding and broken, that transfixed Heart from which was born the Church—all these cruel mysteries of our salvation were already embodied, actually contained, in the first Eucharistic sacrifice.

To the end of time, as priests re-enact the same gestures, as they repeat the same words, the holy liturgy of the Mass as it reaches the moment of the consecration rends space and time, just as the veil of the Temple was rent by the Crucifixion; and that liturgical action links together what it effects and what Jesus effected upon the Cross. This it does directly and unchangingly.

Christians ought, therefore, be mindful of this. In assisting at Mass we are, at the moment of the consecration, present at the blessed death of our Saviour Jesus Christ. Here lies a truth as certain as it is clouded in mystery, a truth which is, as we might say, the cement of our Catholic faith. The Mass is no empty symbol of the Cross, nor is it another sacrifice differing from, as it renews, the sacrifice of the Cross: the Mass is, in very truth, the Cross itself sacramentally borne up before hearts enlightened by faith. In the spirit of Mary Magdalene, these poor souls who are unpreparedly thrown at the foot of the Tree of Life from which sounds the agonized cry of Jesus, should press the cross to their breasts; as did St. John, they should gaze with reverence upon the wound in our Lord's side, the while they share with Mary, the Mother of Jesus, all the pangs of the ignominious death of the most beautiful of the sons of men.

"It is the Lord's death that you are heralding, whenever you eat this bread and drink this cup, until He comes." The Mass is this showing-forth, this manifestation: as the Body and Blood of Jesus are each placed upon the altar as we gaze upon our well-beloved Lord in His redeeming death, our salvation has already begun. That all may adore this mystery, the priest raises the Host, then the Chalice. O Church of Jesus, how well you have guarded this memorial, this act of remembrance which is vitally perpetuated in the Real Presence! *Mihi archiva Christus est!* Jesus crucified sums up the history of His Church!

Thus, the recollection of the Church is wholly focused upon the Passion of Jesus and upon that precious Blood from which the Church took its birth: the sacrifice of Jesus is the lasting treasury of the Church and of Christians, a treasury to which the priesthood has the key. It is to guard and administer this treasury that priests have been anointed, and they seem one with it just as is a mother with the child whom she carries. After the consecrated Host, and alongside of it, it is the priestly heart which, more than anything else in the world, stands as the complete and living continuation and real memorial of Jesus crucified. This is the great memorial for which we must ever be thankful.

The Church's children are baptized only to the end that they may share and communicate in the sacrifice of the Cross: through the priestly ministry each receives its benefits according to his own merits, whether they be of the man having five talents, or three, or one. Of these, the men having five or three talents put them out at interest; but those who have but one bury it in order to keep it secretly against the time when they must render account.

Nothing ought ever succeed in causing us to withdraw ourselves from the unity which is expressed in the Christian sacraments. Yet, even constancy in receiving those sacraments and assiduous attendance at Mass bid fair to make no more than a surface impression on our souls unless we are careful duly to value that with which we are charged. Now, have we actually anything that can really be considered of value to us? Is it possible that we have only succeeded in accumulating a superfluity of external observances which, by becoming separated from their true intention, have lost their efficacy? There is nothing of greater importance to the Christian than that he be mindful of how God so loved him to the end, even to the death of the Cross; it is in the Mass that this mindfulness is best expressed. "I will be mindful," says St. Thomas when writing of the Mass, "I will be mindful of this commemoration, and my soul will yield itself up in love."

We must, therefore, attend Mass with attentive

mindfulness, that is to say, with great faith. Faith is
an infused recollection which is awakened, stimu-
lated, and nourished by the remembrance of Jesus.
Let us grow and increase in our faith. To this end, let
us recommend ourselves to the Blessed Virgin and
to our patron saints. They will help us, so that the
remembrance of the death of the Lord may shine
within us. For it is true of the Mass that it is the
cornerstone linking time and eternity in a wondrous
commingling of love wherein we may absorb, as at
the very source, the merits of Jesus and those of His
saints. The spiritual maternity of Mary, the fatherly
love of St. Dominic, the great fraternal charity of our
patron saints—all are rooted in the Heart of Jesus and
overflow upon us with His redeeming Blood as that
pours through the wound in His side, that wound
which is an everlasting memorial of the great price
at which we were redeemed.

It is of the utmost importance that we understand
that there is but one sacrifice acceptable to God: that
of Jesus; and it continues in actuality, not alone
openly in the rites of the liturgy, but in a mystical
manner in the lives of the penitent and in the precious deaths of those who leave this world in the
state of grace. St. Gregory the Great reminds us that
"when we celebrate the mysteries of the Passion, we
ought to take our share in what we are doing; for, in
respect to ourselves, Jesus is truly and effectively our
Saving Victim before the Father when we share His
sentiments and dispositions and make of ourselves
victims like unto Him." For this reason, when we
are at Mass we must recall not alone the sacrifice of

Jesus, but the compassion of Our Lady, the consecrated lives and deaths of the saints. It is at this time
that we ought to ask to be made members—despite our
unworthiness—of that holy concourse of the blessed,
thinking of it as Fra Angelico has pictured it for us:
a great multitude of souls drawn together by prayer
and holy hope at the foot of the Cross of Jesus.

If we think of the Blessed Virgin, we will realize
how well she has taken care of her treasure and how
—in her virginity and with maternal adoration—she
has guarded the Body and Blood of Jesus whereby
we are redeemed: as offerings already consecrated to
God she had received them, and it is to God that she
ceaselessly offers them in holocaust. May she too
watch over us, guarding us within her motherly heart
and making of us an offering to God in remembrance
of the Passion of Jesus and of her own compassion,
whereby she shared in it.

We know very well that the priesthood and the
Mass were the wellsprings of the loving-kindness of
St. Dominic; that they were to him sources of
strength which never dried up. There is none better
able than he to teach us how to assist at Mass; how
to celebrate it, if we be priests; it is he who will im-
press upon us all how we may, at all times, *live*
the Mass. Let us then, like St. Dominic, with out-
stretched hands crucify all our being as an offering to
God. With faith and with love let us look up at the
Host and the Chalice when the priest raises them
for the adoration of the faithful. Let us affix our souls
and our bodies to Jesus Crucified, offering ourselves in
union with Him by the hands of the priest and plac-

ing our lives and our passing from life on the paten and in the cup.

"The Mass," said St. Vincent Ferrer, "is the very highest kind of contemplation"; and St. Peter of Verona vowed his own blood in a martyr's death as he consecrated the Blood of the Lord.

Devotion to the Mass has been a constant Dominican tradition, and this has shown itself by the establishment of the "Eucharistic Union of the Redeeming Blood," which has its headquarters at Sainte-Baume. This tradition is indeed, like other traditions of the Order, one most deeply Christian. Let us, therefore, under the patronage of St. Mary Magdalene, who was herself present when the Blood of the Redeemer was first poured out, let us learn the true meaning of our Christian calling which is to die daily —*quotidie morior*—sacrificing ourselves in union with the Eucharistic Sacrifice of Jesus. There is no other way in which we are saved but by the Cross. At each Mass in which we participate—and we may share continuously in spirit, as the Mass is celebrated at every hour of the day or night in some part of the world—at each Mass in which we participate, what is asked of us is nothing less than the offering up of our lives, and those immediate fragments of our existence which are this week, this day, this hour. All must be turned entirely to God in an impulse that cuts across all other objects and engages our entire soul.

The world is passing—and the day comes when it will have wholly passed away; we must never lose sight of the fact that the one thing necessary is that we love Jesus Christ. What is there to prevent us from showing that we love Him by constantly offering ourselves to Him in remembrance of and in thanksgiving for His offering of Himself for us? Trouble, sorrow, even death—all afford us only increased opportunities to share more deeply in His blessed Passion. As St. Paul tells us, all things are so ordained that we may never lose sight of the great love of God and His saints, a love stored up for us in those secret treasure-houses of the Mass where Jesus is King.

III

THE ROLE OF THE SAINT IN HUMAN SOCIETY

Translated by
ALASTAIR GUINAN

THE ROLE OF THE SAINT IN HUMAN SOCIETY

We call a *saint* one who is *for* God. Holiness, indeed, implies of its very nature a state of belonging to God, whether it be because of a special consecration, or because of the existence of a moral obligation.

We may speak of the *Holy* Shroud of Turin, or of the *Holy* Places, having in mind their relationship to the person of the Man-God, although this is no more than an attributive relationship, external to the things themselves. When a chalice is consecrated, there is no alteration effected in its nature; but definition is given to its purpose. It is, as a matter of fact, our way of regarding the chalice which has undergone a change: we have set it aside for divine worship. On the other hand, when the destiny or purpose of a man undergoes a change, the whole man is found to have changed. Man and his destiny are closely united. To change his calling is to change the man himself. To set aside a man for God's service is to give to all his work—and even to his very personality—a quality truly divine. If this end be thoroughly defined, the whole life of that man is conducted according to divine leadings. He will truly become a saint. In such a case the end is a radical conformity which leads, as St. John of the Cross puts it, to the union of two natures—the divine and the human—in one subject.

Such conformance to the divine will is possible of realization because it is exercised according to the tendencies or capacities of our nature, enlightened by grace. The choosing of our divine end is something personal and free. No intelligent being makes a true and defined choice of end unless that choice be knowing and free. Someone who is not free is not holy, cannot be holy or in any manner capable of the kind of holiness of which I speak, a holiness which gives up to God the full right to make use of the spiritual being. The saint does not trample upon his liberty: he accomplishes its entire fulfilment in God. What he wills is what God wills; he turns aside from all that is unpleasing to God. It is the most precious characteristic within him—his liberty—that is so directed that it tends toward, and culminates in, God.

We have an example of holiness of an even higher order in that bond whereby Christ is united to God. In Him sanctity, instead of being merely a characteristic of action and tendency, is one of the basic notes of His being. Christ is holiness personified: His sanctity inheres in His very substance. The bond which unites Him to God is a bond of nature in which They are Father and Son yet both, identically, God. No sacrilege, no sin, can ever destroy this union in the way in which the holy purpose of a chalice can be set at naught if it be broken; it is the indivisible Trinity Itself which would first have to be split apart. Christ as man is all-holy; all His acts and words are holy, not alone because they tend toward God, but because they come from God as their sole and immediate author. They had no need of special consecration to divine service, they had no need of a choice to make them tend toward God. His consecration and entire direction of life and being to the Father's will date, in the human Jesus, from the very moment of His conception in the womb of the Immaculate Virgin who is the Mother of God. In Him, human nature was totally restored to its supreme capacity, and this was done in a special manner in accordance with His divine destiny.

Now that God, by the Incarnation, had taken upon Himself our human nature, sanctity or holiness became much easier and more certain of realization by us; now far readier to our hand. We have but to imitate the deeds of the God-Man to follow His example, to obey His commandments and counsels, and conform ourselves to Him in order to fulfill with certainty our work or function in the divine plan. Holiness has in Him become Christian. Just as an apple tree brings forth apples, so are saints the fruit of the imitation of Christ. The problem of our supernatural destiny is summed up in the place which Christ has in our lives. It is Christ who gives us a sense of God's majesty. All those men or women whom the Church has canonized have this in common, regardless of what places they may have held in life: they were wholly given over to following Christ in the service of God. In their own eyes these men and women were no more than lowly members of Jesus Christ; they thought of themselves as the unworthy servants of the God for whom they labored. This is why they are saints. And it is for this reason that they are honored by the Catholic Church who holds them up before us that we may venerate and follow them.

Actually, there is nothing absolute about the ven-

eration of the saints; it is entirely a matter of rela-
tivity. It is only because of the confusion created by
Protestantism and rigorism that it becomes necessary
to stress truisms. Needless to say, God alone—and
Christ because He is God—is worthy of total worship, directed to Himself and for Himself. This is
what the theologians call *the cult of latria,* that is,
worship properly so called. It is only by reason of
their union with God and Christ that the Blessed
Virgin and the saints are honored. A perfect analogy
exists in the fact that the images of kings are held
in high respect; for sanctity is a kind of conformity
or resemblance to God. And things are even simpler
than this example would imply. God loves His saints.
In the great Christian family they are His favorite
children. His loving heart would have us, too, share
in the love which He has for them, and in that
particular affection in which He holds His Mother.

Whether it rest upon the Church triumphant or
upon us who still struggle here below, it is the self-
same heritage—the friendship of God—that the
saints enjoy in the revelation of glory and that we
grasp by the mysterious help of grace. And we are
sons of the saints by virtue of the mystical blood
which flows from their souls into our hearts. St.
Thomas Aquinas had been the pupil of St. Albertus
Magnus. When Thomas died at an early age, Albert
betook himself to Paris in order to defend before the
doctors of the Sorbonne the memory and the teaching of Thomas, his former pupil, then under severe
criticism. In what was, at that time, the foremost uni-
versity of the world he spoke as Professor of Divinity,

and said: "Of what avail is it that one who lives should be praised by the dead?" Now the saints in heaven are alive for evermore. How foolish to think that the closeness of the saints to God removes them from us, or that their interest in us could separate them from God! Had we known them on earth we would certainly have been impressed by their heroic virtue; we would have asked for their help and for their prayers, on our behalf, to the God they served so faithfully, that they would beg Him to give us His grace. We would have experienced great happiness in knowing and in being with St. Paul, St. Dominic, or St. Jeanne d'Arc. Who can tell what it would mean to see them, to clasp their hands, to beg them for their loving aid, and to receive the fruits of their friendship? Well, all these good things, represented by the friendship of the saints, are easily available: they are stored up for us in the Heart of Jesus, King and Center of all hearts, burning brightly with the ardent fire of love; all are to be had at the price of our prayer and our good-will. Stretching over the abyss of our mortal lives and of our earthly death, the saints reach out their hands as they guide us along the road of destiny which we tread as children of God.

Surely we would have loved the saints. . . . We may be certain that they would have loved us, their charity being of an all-enveloping delicacy in precision of selectiveness. St. Francis of Assisi loved even the animals, and for them he delivered sermons to which they listened. Would we have listened? And can we be certain that we would really have loved the saints? The saints help us not only to return to God,

but also they incite in us profound thoughts about the
exact point to which our destiny tends; they help us to
realize whether or not we are actually leading Christian lives. Before they came to share in the glory of
Jesus they had been partakers of His sufferings. There
are countless details in their lives which must give us
pause, for they suggest questions to us which are dis-
turbing to our complacency, questions, moreover,
which refuse to be put aside. The saints shared in the
sufferings of Jesus; they perpetuate among men the
Passion of Christ, that each may know whether he belongs by the side of Judas, or of Peter the denier, or of
Pilate, or, mayhap, of the Pharisees, or of the Good
Thief stretched upon a cross.

Ah! yes; the great question which they raise—a
question more embarrassing than it may seem—is
precisely the question: *Would we really have loved
them?* For, after all, those, for instance, who judged
Jeanne d'Arc were not monsters. Learned men and
well intentioned, they were deeply concerned about
the maintenance of law and of established order. It was
they who wrote to the Pope: "If things are come to
such a pass that sorceresses may falsely teach in the
name of God, as a certain female has done, who is
now held captive in Beauvais, and if such teaching
take hold upon the public fancy in preference to the
authority of priests and scholars, then without doubt
shall we see religion perish and the faith wither away;
the Church will be brought low, and it is the misrule
of Satan that will reign throughout the land." It is by
no means certain that we might not have found ourselves on the side of those who judged Jeanne d'Arc,

rather than among the supporters of "popular fancy." At least, it is very likely that we might have been in the position of Charles VII, who forsook the Maid. We are taught by the saints how difficult it is to be satisfied before God that we are on "the right side."

With wonderful psychological insight, the Church arouses us each morning by pricking our conscience with the recollection of a saint who is made a part of our life for that day. In this connection, there comes to mind a little story imagined by Péguy:

"Once upon a time there was a man who was very bored, so dreadfully bored . . . it is impossible to describe how bored the man was. His life was so dreary, so dull, so gloomy, that his whole occupation, each day, was boredom. But this man who was always bored the whole day long, this man who was bored in the morning, bored in the evening, knew that to arouse himself from his boredom he need only commit a serious sin. There occurred to him a really serious sin, enormous, gigantic, a sin which would—at least for once—deliver him from his ennui. It would be a sin without peer.

"To commit this sin it was only necessary that he write a letter; nothing but a letter. He need only take a sheet of paper, set it before him upon his desk, dip his pen in the inkwell, write, blot it, seal it, attach the stamp, and drop the letter in the post box. That would do it, once for all. He would have done something in his life. How often had he said: 'No; it would be too crazy in the long run; I would be too bored!' He had always stopped in time.

"Now a day came when the life of this poor man was even more boring than usual, and he struggled no longer. 'Come on . . . ,' said he. And he took up a piece of letter paper. But I must tell you that this bored man was in the grip of a mania which asserted itself whenever he wrote. He was unable to look at the date without at the same time taking note of the saint whose day it was. 'Come, come . . . ,' said he, taking down the calendar. 'Saturday the 21st, Sunday the 22nd, Monday the 23rd, Tuesday the 24th, Wednesday the 25th; Good—St. Louis.'

"St. Louis, ah! things won't be so smooth! St. Louis. He chewed his moustache. St. Louis. Truly, he lacked courage to commit a serious sin on St. Louis' day. It would be impossible. There was no use in even dreaming of it. Think now of St. Louis and all he stands for: Blanche of Castille; St. Louis dispensing justice; St. Louis and the Crusades; St. Louis at Carthage; his sword; his scepter; his bed of ashes; St. Louis, king of France, model, exemplar, and patron of the kings of France. He stands for all of ancient France, he the Protector of France and of Frenchmen, wearing his fine blue robe sewn with fleurs-de-lys and carrying the rod of justice, as in the painting by old Laurens. It would be impossible to go on. Never would St. Louis let him do such a thing as he contemplated.

"You see the point: the idea, the recollection, the notion of St. Louis being present in his thoughts was sufficient to stop him at once. The saints of France—and especially St. Louis—are saints who get under one's skin. Such is St. Louis.

"But things would not so prolong themselves. The

bored man put the calendar back in its place, saying
to himself that it was no more than a question of de-
laying what he would do. He had decided. The more
he waited, the wearier he grew. He must have done
with it. St. Louis. Rain, wind, sun, his acquaintances,
his wife, his friends, the day, the night, whatever he
did, or what he might have done—all bored him. But
St. Louis.

"The next day, he tore open his box of letter paper,
carefully spread a sheet from it on his desk, plunged
his pen into the inkwell. 'Ah! the date—Wednesday,
Thursday the 26th, St. Zephyrinus. Ah! St. Zephyrinus. Good. Good!' And he begins to write.

"All at once there is a little man who strikes him
a blow on the nose, like a strong current of wind; for
you know how tremendous a gust the Greek zephyr
can be. The little man is furious; his face reddens in
rage, as he says: 'How now, what goes on here? Yesterday, you wouldn't dare commit your sin because it
was the feast of St. Louis. Today, you are ready for it
because it is only the day of St. Zephyrinus. He counts
for nothing. That is the reason I have come. This is a
fine thing. You wouldn't dare commit your sin yesterday, even though you wanted to, because you are
afraid of St. Louis. St. Louis, the king, the greatest
king of them all. Today, however, is only my day, the
day of a little scrap of a saint who counts for nothing.
I ask you, what is St. Zephyrinus indeed? You can get
away with anything, as far as he is concerned. Just because it's only my day, you are quite ready to throw
yourself into hell. That's fine. You have it all worked
out. St. Zephyrinus. Not on your life.' In short, the lit-

tle saint had so much to say that back into the box
went the writing paper.

"But the man who was bored became more and
more decided upon writing the letter. His desire
turned to obstinacy. The next day, he opened his box
and went through the same rigmarole—paper, ink,
pen, date, calendar. Ah! St. Damian. St. Damian—he
meant nothing to him. He scanned the room, peer-
ing into its corners; turned his head two or three
times, glancing around himself; but he saw nothing.
He plunged his pen into the inkwell. Bang! Crash! All
at once St. Damian is before him. And he is not alone.
His brother, St. Cosmas, is with him. As a pair they
are stronger; two great saints; two great saints even
though this man doesn't know it. They are carrying
the instruments of their martyrdom, and St. Damian
remarks in a sad voice: 'Then it's all decided. The day
before yesterday, you gave way to St. Louis, and yesterday you deferred to St. Zephyrinus. Today—on my
day—you are ready to insult me. What will they say
to me in heaven? What do you think St. Peter will
say? I can hear him now: "You have certainly done
good work on your day! You've let this stupid man
fall into the arms of his sin. For twenty-four hours
you're asked to watch over the world, and how have
you done it? There's nothing left to say." Come, my
friend, yield to one good inspiration; give me that
paper and say a little prayer to your holy patron, my
colleague, that he will help you.'

"So it was every day. The bored man was obstinate,
but the saints showed themselves obstinate, too.
Some appealed to him kindly: 'Please, please don't

do this to a little saint like me; you really don't want to. Please tell me that you don't.' And he stopped because he felt sorry for them. Other saints—teachers, theologians, learned scholars, scholastics and neo-scholastics—put the case to him with such an array of logic and syllogisms that they proved to him the danger of the action he contemplated. And so they left him convinced. Others berated him sharply; these were the soldiers among the saints: St. George, St. Martin, St. Charlemagne. They did not let him off easily. He actually remained quite good for two whole days, so frightened was he after that formidable French sovereign had invaded his room, accompanied by two of his vassals—as in the sculptured group on the square before Notre Dame de Paris—and had carried off his letter paper, his pen, and his ink, after turning the place upside down.

"Thus was he rebuffed on all sides. But he would not give in. He thought that in order to go through with his intention of sinning, he would do well to go away from Paris; for in leaving town for the country he fancied that he might attract less notice there. Now it became a different matter: it was no longer the saint of the day whom he would insult, but the patrons of parishes who guard the entry to their domains. There were bearded saints who had themselves lived in the forests, saints never heard of in the city calendars; peasant saints, protectors of wood-choppers and their huts, saints who kept an eye on growing things to guard them from frost, rain, and storm. He was faced with one after another of these saints at the crossroads or before the churches he passed. There were jolly saints who guarded their flocks; great lords who had fled the world and who were satisfied to govern the happiness of shepherds; the kind of saints who, above all things, disliked to see things upset.

"So it was that he was unable to commit his serious sin.

"You see now what I want you to see. All that I have said is to make you see—mark it well—that there is no part of the earth or any point in the life of a Christian wherein he ceases, even for one minute, to be guarded and watched over by the special protection of the saints."[1]

Now, it seems to me that this tale of Péguy's points out very clearly the way in which the hagiographical tradition of the Church is to be understood. Rather than offering to us a quantity of documented history, this tradition conveys a sense of perceptible presence, the presence of those clouds of witnesses in the heavens of whom St. Paul speaks, and in whose sight we live and die. A view of the saints is conveyed rather after the fashion of a good portrait painter than in the manner of the photographer. Some details are legendary. Yet they are, nevertheless, details of outstanding religious value. They transcribe, in symbolic fashion, religious truths which are in themselves quite certain. Legends may be compared to the cinema in its power of telescoping events occurring on different planes, and in the open and acknowledged trickery by which it prolongs or hastens the point of the story. Legend is an accumulation—a gathering-up—of truths of different orders. The result is something extraordinarily

[1] Quoted by René Johannet.

suggestive; and in this suggestiveness we are offered the grace of God through the splendid achievements of His saints.

Moreover, it is beside the point to think that this entire tradition is historically false. I would suggest that, even were such the case, the materials have been put together less with didactic intent than as a kind of poetic incantation, as a sort of mood-setter, by which the soul rather than the intelligence is to open itself to supernatural influence. Herein lies the usefulness of the saints. We do not need to know very much about them: the important thing is to follow them, to grasp the hands they hold out to us, to allow ourselves to be led by them into those hidden paths of the spiritual life in which they first walked as pioneers.

"Our Church is the Church of saints! To be a saint, what bishop would not give up his ring, his miter, and his staff, what cardinal would not relinquish his purple, or what pope his white robe, his chamberlains, his guards, and all his temporal power? Who does not wish for strength to carry on in this wonderful adventure? For the quest of sanctity is an adventure, it is really the only true adventure.

"Whosoever understands this has penetrated to the very center of the Catholic faith, and he feels trembling within his mortal fiber a terror other than the fear of death—a hope which is more than human. Our Church is the Church of saints. Yet, who concerns himself overmuch with them? It might be wished that they had been old men politically experienced; and the greater number are only children. Now, a child stands alone against all. The malicious shrug their shoulders and laugh: what saint has much to praise about churchmen and what are churchmen doing here anyhow? God has not made the Church for the earthly welfare of the saints, but that it might preserve their memory, lest that memory be lost together with their divine gift, a torrent of honor and of poetry.

"Let another Church show its saints! Ours is the Church of saints. To whom else would you entrust this angelic band? History, in its brief manner, has broken them to fit the narrow and constricted columns of its bare narration. Our Catholic tradition has embraced them unhurt, and lovingly gathers them into its all-appealing rhythm: St. Benedict and his raven, St. Francis with his mandolin and his love for the songs of Provence, Jeanne d'Arc and her sword, Vincent in his shabby soutane, and—more recently—Thérèse of the Child Jesus with her incomprehensible smile, besieged by traffickers in spiritual things. Would these saints have wished, while they were alive, to be enthroned, smothered with overblown salutations, and greeted with genuflections and clouds of incense? Such gestures are all very well when they are directed toward the canons' stalls. The saints lived and suffered in their time as we do in ours. They had their work to do; and more than one of them, rather than leave it, laid down under its burden and died. Those who do not yet dare to follow their example will at least learn from them lessons about heroism and honor. But who would not blush to stop here, and leave them to go forth alone? Who would wish to lose his life by ruminating upon the problem of evil rather than by throwing himself into the effort to save that life? Who would refuse to set humanity free?" [2]

When the theologians have sought to discern more closely that degree of union with God which they call holiness or sanctity, they have described it as possessing two qualities: purity and strength.

In respect to certain material adjuncts to sacred worship, these qualities are in fact required in the fashion proper to that object's holiness, that is to say they are required in a juridical sense. The interior of a chalice's cup must be gilt, gold being esteemed as a pure and precious metal. In the same way, despite the fact that crystal is also a pure and precious material, its use for a chalice will not be permitted, inasmuch as it lacks the required strength.

When we rise to the consideration of a holiness which is spiritual rather than juridical, of that kind of holiness which is, properly speaking, that to which human beings are called, those qualities are found to be internal and spiritual; and they are called properties or characteristics of the sanctity from which they flow.

Sanctity is that definition of purpose which sets the end of being in God. No soul can approach God unless it make itself pure. God is, as the philosophers tell us, *Actus purus* or Pure Act, that is to say, He is exempt from every limitation or susceptibility to change. His infinity is the full completeness of entire reality. As St. Paul tells us, He is like a devouring fire; and it is

[2] Bernanos, *Jeanne relapse et sainte,* pp. 61-4.

out of the question that any soul come close to God and fail to react to this flame. "The heart of the saint is fluid," said the Curé d'Ars. This fluidity is not like that of dish water which gathers up all sorts of soiled matter: it is rather to be compared to that of the hardest metals as they react to the electric ray. There exists no heart so firm that God cannot cleanse it of every alloy. Herein doubtless lies the secret of purgatory and also the secret of holiness here below. God cannot allow us to do without purgatory, for purgatory is the fiery path to Him. The sooner, therefore, that we suffer, the better will it be. Such is the lesson of the saints.

The attraction of God to the soul is the cause of the soul's right ordering of all its desires. He satisfies it in drawing it to Him; He leads it on, He enlightens it by giving it beauty and brilliancy. Souls are beautiful in the measure in which they reflect the image of God of whom they have been made mirrors; and those mirrors gain in clarity as they more truly show forth His holy face. Holiness is not so much a matter of wishing "to perfect oneself" as it is a matter of desiring God, His kingdom, and His justice. All the rest is granted by way of increase, all the rest; so comes that purity which is the true beauty of the soul. Purity is then a thing of positive nature: it consists in union with the center and source of all purity, God Himself. Therefore, in human holiness it becomes rather an effect of holiness than a condition of the state, as is the case in the juridical holiness which we ascribe to things and objects used in liturgical worship.

God is the immutable Center of all things. In that universal gravitation of souls, every soul is restless until it finds its repose in Him. The love of God is the deep plumb of balance of the spiritual being. The more the soul yields to that love, the more fixed and certain it becomes. Care must be taken, however, that stagnation be avoided; for it is only in heaven that the soul will be so firmly joined to its Center that no sundering of it from God will be possible. On earth the fixity of a holy soul is a matter of it being oriented toward God with ever-increasing exactness and strength. This may be compared to the way in which the velocity, the dynamic density, and the tendency to verge toward its center increases, moment by moment, in a stone which has fallen from a great height. Inflexibility of soul is a growing certainty of its upward flight. It is also an effect of holiness, of the determined orientation of the soul toward God.

At this point in our investigation it will be of interest to compare the saint with the hero. In ancient mythology the birth of the hero is always ascribed to the union of a god and a woman, or of a goddess and a man. As with the saint, the origin of the hero is thought of as joining the divine and the human; but the meaning of the two attitudes is nevertheless quite different. In his origin the hero of classic times *surpassed* man: he was *superman,* and his destiny lay in the performance of mighty deeds, worthy of his origin. The only element of humanity which remained in him was the result of the mesalliance of his parents: it induced in him a consequent incapacity to be *fully* an inheritor of the divine.

Christ, however, is in no wise a mixture of the divine and the human. In the transcendent and infinite unity of His personality, divine nature and human nature blend harmoniously into the perfect wholeness of each. Christ has human intelligence, human will, and human liberty. In Him divinity is not an element which unseats human nature. On the contrary, it rather restores it wonderfully to its own essential equilibrium. Christ is no superman. He is a man, of the same nature of any one of us, although in Him a special grace brings to their fullness all the gifts of human nature. And at the same time Christ is God in person, having suffered no lessening of His divine nature. Christ—apart from His miracles, which are to be ascribed to the divine omnipotence which dwelt in Him rather than to any classic *heroicity*—Christ was not called to display superhuman deeds: He lived and died a very human life and death. Yet, the very slightest of His human actions was perfect, the result of complete freedom of choice and action, and wholly centered in God, and was of infinite value, because it was the Son of God who functioned in this integral human nature, at the same time respecting all its essential qualities.

In imitation of Jesus, the saint is no superman. His heroism—like that of Christ—is human. After the time of Christ heroism has been demonstrated in two ways—that of the stoic and that of the Christian; and there is nothing more unlike Christianity than stoicism of heart and spirit. The saint is a man like you and me, one in whom the grace of God works, not after the fashion of a manipulator of marionettes pulling strings, but rather through an intimate penetration of the soul and its faculties which at the same time strengthens the free functioning of those faculties. The saint is no God-driven automaton. He is the friend of God, the child of God; it is the man who functions; but he does so for the love of God. The saints in heaven are yet men, but men in whom dwells the glory of God.

It is the stoic hero who fashions his own statue; but it is God who works upon the saint from within, always respecting that lowly human creature whom He has made, whom He knows and loves. God indeed loves man and wishes him well. He wills Himself to be man's human joy, in the sense that He has put something of Himself in man—together with His own indescribable likeness—a capacity for, an openness to, the infinite.

The hero of antiquity knew his superhuman origin; and he wished to live up to it by performing deeds beyond the power of men. The saint knows that he is the brother of Jesus Christ, and that the kingdom of heroism is also within him. He wills that his whole life be modeled upon the human life of his Lord. The honor of the stoic is based upon his own nobility. The saint owns no other honor than that of God. But he knows that his honor is also in his personal charge, because he is the son of God by grace. He knows this honor to be bound up with his least task here on earth; he knows that this honor is confided to our mortal hands, and that it suffers in some manner according to the vicissitudes of our Christian fidelity. If we are able to give honor to God, it is in the same degree that we are able to dishonor Him.

Like the honor of the saint, that of the hero is characterized by purity and fixity. The hero has no wish to do anything unworthy of himself; he turns aside from all that would mar or stain his glory and the good opinion he has of himself. The saint knows himself unworthy of God. He knows, too, the commandment of Christ: "But you are to be perfect, as your heavenly Father is perfect"; he knows that God loves us and that this love purifies and transforms us. The hero strives and works for himself; the saint works for God, and this supernatural impetus evokes in him powers of heroism which classic antiquity did not even dream existed in man. The fixity of the hero is a harsh observance. The firmness of the saint is a bondage of love. The stoic has sometimes even to clinch his teeth in order to maintain his high standard. The saint knows that God loves the sinner and that He ceaselessly holds out to him His grace, urging him to repent. The faces of the saints may even be sad, sometimes to the point of agony; but they are never constrained. It would be a great misfortune if an overly ascetic idea of sanctity fathered us with young Christians after the pattern of Epictetus and Plutarch, sermonizing and rigid as justice instead of possessing the attractiveness of charity.

Moreover, it is difficult to fix in the heart of Christianity a standard of heroic living grounded entirely on the moral level. There is indeed a Christian heroism, but its font is theological rather than moral. It is not animated by the hero's regard for personal eminence, but by a realization of God's majesty. The heroism of the saint is not established by strongly taking oneself in hand, but by placing oneself in the hands of God. St. Paul has told us that it is a fearsome thing to fall into the hands of the living God. Let those who think that Christianity implies a withdrawal from life look at the saints. They will learn how costly it is to man to yield himself loyally to all the exactions of God's friendship.

Not all Christians are saints. Not all are on the way to becoming saints. One may accept loyally and in all actuality the hazards of companionship with that God who will have none other put before Him, or one may play with the notion. We have all observed the rapid growth of the kind of human weed we call the *devotee*. What exactly is a devotee in this sense? It goes without saying that I am not using the word in its elevated and proper theological sense, as we encounter it in the writings of St. Francis de Sales. I am taking it rather in the popular contemporary sense: this is always pejorative, with the connotation *pietistic*.

Such a devotee is a would-be saint who desires merely sanctity, whereas a saint seeks God. The devotee seeks a sanctity of which he has a static and materialistic concept. He fancies, whether or not he acknowledges it even to himself, that one may become a saint on the strength of some extrinsic consecration or blessing like the rites and formalities which set aside a chalice or a chasuble for liturgical use. He thinks that holiness comes about independently of his own free will and choice, and without the trouble

entailed by a deep and radical reforming of his own
inner nature, resulting in a complete turning of the
self to God.

St. Thomas Aquinas has explained very clearly how
superstition may easily creep into the religion of
Christians if that religion be allowed to express itself
solely by exercises and ceremonies without regard to
the inner worship of the spirit, which is faith, hope,
and charity. The devotee has an inclination to this
sort of false religion. His concept of Christian salvation is overly materialistic and, as a matter of fact, not
human enough. He knows nothing of that *rationabile
obsequium*—that reasonable service or free filial submission—of which St. Paul speaks. Urgent concern for
the honor of God purifies and strengthens the saint.
The devotee, however, is more apt to concentrate
upon purity or security in himself than on the
honor of God. His basic motivation is in his fear. He
fears hell; he fears the renunciations which mark the
calling of a Christian; he fears to set aside human respect, he tries to skirt all dangers without being
ensnared by any of them, just as a canoe shoots the
rapids of a river. It might be said of him that he is ever
inclined to convert the Christian axiom, "One must
work out his own salvation," into the profoundly un-
Christian and inhuman, "Every man for himself." His
fear of taking a chance leads to avarice. Now, the saint,
on the other hand, spends himself without ceasing, so
that he may give his whole life to God. The devotee
schemes and plans to avoid the slightest expenditure
of self, the least experience of suffering in either this
world or the next. He gambles, indeed, on holiness;
but his gambling is always very careful, like that of

those cold gamesters who play roulette to the limit
of ten francs each Sunday, but who despise one who
would allow himself to be ruined by a passionate love
of gambling.

The devotee goes just so far in sin. He never burns
his boats. The sacrament of Penance appears to him as
a way in which he may easily reckon up the balance
sheet of his evil deeds, whenever his good standing in
the sight of God appears definitely uncertain, and
achieve once more a clean slate. The devotee is re-
markably astute, for he can dispense himself from the
obligations incumbent upon members of human society by invoking supernatural privileges, while at the
same time he will plead the duties of his temporal
state in order to excuse his disregard for the stricter
construction of the Gospel call to repentance. He is
as busy as the beaver who builds his dwelling place in
the piles of a dock, and is thus equally at the mercy
of the hazards of land and water. And after all this,
what? In such an existence where is there room for
the Cross of Christ?

The saint, however, will plunge headlong into the
doing of God's will, even if that require that he lose
all and suffer all. Insofar as his eternal destiny is concerned, he places it wholly in God's hands. In that
gracious wholehearted and explicit expression of his
acceptance of God's will of which St. Paul and other
saints have given us examples, he declares that even
the contradiction of damnation would be acceptable
to him could such be the divine decision.

The most obvious consequence of the devotee's attitude is a frightening loss of humanity. This is easy to
understand, for the devotee does not give himself

wholly to anything he does, and human nature is fulfilled only when it functions like the seed which is
planted in the earth. This is the true sense of the parable of the talents. The devotee prefers to make the
least possible use of his liberty lest he lose it. "Truly,"
says Christ, "he who does not gather his store with
me, scatters it abroad." It is in the practice of the love
of God that the saint discovers a refined sense of courtesy and of human brotherhood, while God Himself
receives the soul wholly given up to Him and, by
giving Himself in return, grants that soul its true fulfilment.

To the evil-doer the problem of man presents itself
in a different fashion. I speak here of the evil-doer not
as the man who commits what seems to him a useful
crime, or who acts when in the grip of anger, but
rather as the kind of evil-doer whom Dostoievski, for
one, has described, a man who deliberately and know-
ingly is set upon evil.

"It was my wish, Sonia, simply to kill, just for myself alone, for my own sake. I have no desire to lie
about this, even to myself. . . . I have simply killed,
killed for my own sake, for myself alone. . . . Would
I leap the barrier or would I not dare? This was the
question I put to myself: Am I a creature of fear,
or can I take it upon myself to do this? . . . Listen to
how I set out for the old woman's house, just that I
might see how things would go. . . ." The evil-doer,
so defined, puts himself in the place of God. The eternal law seems to him only as a barrier to be sur-
mounted *in order to be himself*. He wants to have his
action measured solely by his will to accomplish it.

He makes of it an absolute, a self-justifying entity. In the fullest sense of the words, he puts himself beyond the law, beyond all law. As a matter of fact, he exalts his own deed to the point of constituting it the law. This is wholly due to his contemptuousness and his pride. ". . . And, Sonia, now I know that anyone who is strong in mind and spirit is the master of men. Anyone who is greatly daring is right in their eyes. He who despises most things will be a lawgiver among them and he who dares most of all will be most in the right. So it has always been; so it will always be. One would have to be blind, not to see it." [8]

The similarity between evil-doer and saint lies in the fact that both one and the other carry to the end what their hearts dictate. They press on intrepidly to the act. Neither is a mere dreamer. The saint is wholly the creature of his love, as the evil-doer is of his own contemptuousness. But whereas love brings all to fruition, in contemptuousness all is blighted. The evil-doer is unable to accept even the exactions of his own existence, he has to commit suicide in order to demonstrate his mastery of his own being.

Herein lies the mystic confrontation between the law—all law—and human freedom. It might easily seem that law contradicts this freedom; yet the saint believes—and he proves—that it may be its affirmation. In effect, love possesses the power of blending two wills into one, and of doing this in a real and living fashion. By loving God with all his heart, the saint goes beyond the law, even as he fulfils it. This it was that Christ said: "I have not come to set aside [the

[8] *Crime and Punishment*, Part 2, chap. 4.

law] but to bring it to perfection," to complete it, to bring it to its true fruition, which is love; to extract from it its highest end, which is freedom. The saint, by love, makes himself one with the Supreme Law-giver. The law is no longer an obstacle or barrier to him, for it has become the instrument whereby he may the more effectively and concretely prove his love. "Now the soul is at liberty; it has the keys of entry. It has passed through the door. It may go in and out and find places of fulfillment." It would not even be more exact to say that the ability to discern had been increased; for it is in the infinite fullness of spir-itual freedom that there runs the *strait path:* "Now there is no further journeying. And for the holy there is no more law." [4] The saint is outside the law, but this is so because he is one with God. And when he is no longer in a state of contemplative union, he is under the shelter of the law in easy freedom; for it is the ex-pression of his own life, there being in him no other principle of life than the love of God. In loving, one wills what is willed by the object of that love. "Love," says St. Paul, "fulfills all the demands of the law." One might turn this expression around by saying that for the saint the law is the overflowing fulfilment of his free love of God. It is thus that St. Thomas Aquinas has magnificently expressed the idea: "When the Holy Spirit by his love turns our will in the direction of the true end to which it naturally tends, he frees us from that bondage which makes us slaves of passion and sin and constrains us to act contrary to the very nature of the will. And he frees us, too, from that other slavery in which we strive against the very

---

[4] Maritain, *Distinguer pour unir; Todo y nada.*

movement of his divine will and become no longer his friends but the mere obeyers of his law." So has St. Paul said, "Where the Lord's Spirit is, there is freedom," and again, "It is by letting the Spirit lead you that you free yourselves from the yoke of the law."

At this point in holiness, the sharing of life with God is realized in a sharing of all good, and the saint both by nature and by grace partakes in God's lordship over the universe. Holiness is the end at which all law aims, and everything that is belongs to the chosen of God, for it is for their sake that He has willed and made all that exists. "Mine are the heavens and mine is the earth; all men, just and sinners alike, are mine. The angels are mine, and the Mother of God, and all else beside. Even God himself is mine and for me; because Christ is mine and wholly for me. And now, O my soul, what more do you seek or ask? All is yours and all is wholly for you!" [5]

★ ★ ★

While retaining our chosen point of concern—the role of the saint in human society—about which all these remarks converge, I would like now to touch upon a complicated facet of the whole problem. This lies in the question of the difference between the saints from the human viewpoint. We are counselled by the author of *Imitation* not to seek to determine who is greater among the saints. This is good advice, and there is no question, here, of going counter to it. The declaration by the Church that a saint is a saint assures us of his heavenly glory. The Church holds all saints up for our imitation, for they all re-

[5] St. John of the Cross.

flect, in varying ways, the one real holiness which is
that of the Lord Jesus. The saints are saints precisely
for the reason that they show a likeness to God and to
Christ. This conformity of theirs is accepted by us all,
and there is here no intention of even raising a question about it.

So much said, it follows that, in imitating the saints,
we are able to make our own choice of models. It is
thus purposely that I have stressed so much the real
nature of the humanity of the saints, in contrast to
the qualities of the superman. Our own life is also
an actual human life of which we must give an account before God when He calls us to be judged. It is
this same lowly human life that Christ has redeemed
at the price of His Blood; it is this same life which the
saints help us to lead in conformity with the stirrings
of God's grace. What we must lay open to the grace
which streams from the Cross is the totality of our
actual lives, not some disembodied dream about them
which floats, as it were, above the realities of existence. Leaving aside any consideration of the theological virtues of the saints, it may be observed that each
saint has his own temperament, his own state in life;
his personal abilities, his characteristic spirit and the
feeling proper to his own heart, his own place in time
and space. All this observable variation of circum-
stances may result in one saint or another being more
or less close, and more or less sympathetic—hence
more or less useful—to one or another of us. An example will afford a real explanation of the differences
of which I speak.

St. Alphonsus de'Liguori was an Italian nobleman

of the eighteenth century. In his early years he became an attorney in his native town. His career gave promise of being a brilliant one, and his father, Don Giuseppe de'Liguori, wanted him to make an advantageous marriage. But Alphonsus was already so much inclined to the service of God that he had privately resolved to lead a life of perfect celibacy. Nevertheless, he suffered' all arrangements for a betrothal to be made by his father; and, according to the pious writer of his life, whom I now quote, this is how he extricated himself from the engagement:

"Always on the alert in the making of connections that would redound to the honor of his own family, he [Don Giuseppe] now planned the marriage of Alphonsus with the daughter of the Duke of Presenzano. The first stage of the negotiations having gone off well, many receptions, parties, and similar gatherings were held, and the young lawyer put a good face upon the matter in order to avoid annoying his father. . . . He merely showed himself indifferent to the young princess.

"This coldness did not escape the observant eye of Don Giuseppe, and he accordingly descanted most eloquently upon the education, the fine mind, the piety, and the attractiveness of the young lady. He spoke of the high rank of her parents, the benefits which such a marriage would bring to his family, and of all sorts of other reasons favorable to the match. Without openly refusing his own consent to marrying the girl, Alphonsus alluded to his ill health which he said made him averse to marriage. Don Giuseppe shrugged his shoulders, and continued his visits to the Palazzo Presenzano. His son accompanied him, despite his own feelings; but he showed so much reserve, so much circumspection, that it might have been seen that each man went rather to please the other than himself. So extremely strained a situation could not long endure.

"One evening, as conversation came to a standstill, they looked to music to pass the time. The artistic talent of Alphonsus was well known to all, and therefore the duke and several other gentlemen invited him to play the harpsichord. He graciously agreed. After he had brilliantly played several selections, the daughter of the duke suggested that he accompany her singing of a ballad. She stood near Alphonsus and turned her face toward him. Continuing to play, he turned his own head in the opposite direction, out of modesty. Misunderstanding the reason for his action, the young princess left the place where she was and went to the other side of the player. Once again her accompanist turned his head away and this put the singer so out of countenance that she left the room in vexation, declaring: 'This man seems to me to be slightly crazy.' After this occurrence, although her parents tried to convince her of the young man's good qualities and the advantages of the marriage, she did not want to hear any more about it." [6]

Now, four centuries earlier, in Italy also, although it is true it was in Tuscany, the same situation was handled in a very different fashion by a young girl of sixteen, Catherine of Siena. This story unfolds a scene of much popular appeal. The mother of Catherine had

[6] Père Berthe, *Saint Alphonse de Liguori.*

made up her mind that her daughter should marry, and an argument arose which suddenly flared up loudly between them.

"Catherine must marry!"

"Catherine will never marry!"

And the young miss went up to her room, shaved off all her hair, and then came back to her mother and declared:

"Catherine will never marry!"

How much more easily one breathes in this kind of atmosphere!

However, there is in the life of this same Catherine of Siena another episode which is startling in many ways, and which serves to show even more the human differences between the saints. I would ask the reader to keep in mind the picture of Alphonsus de'Liguori at the harpsichord and the actions of himself and of others in the story, retaining the whole as part of a diptych to be set alongside another scene in Catherine's life, as told by herself. The tale has to do with a young man of Perugia, aged twenty, called Niccolò Tuldo. For some slight offense this boy had been condemned to death by the rulers of Siena. Disgusted by the cruelty of the sentence, Tuldo returned to his cell like a caged wolf; he cursed the name of God and he refused to see a priest. Catherine was told about the matter, and this is what she wrote to the Dominican Raymond of Capua:

"I went to see the man you know of. He found in my visit so much consolation and solace that he went to confession and has now composed his soul. He made me promise, for the love of God, that I would stand near him at the time of his execution. This I promised, and this have I done. Early in the morning, before the bells were rung, I went to see him, and this greatly comforted him. I saw to it that he assisted at Mass; he received Holy Communion, which he had hitherto refused. His will was now rightly disposed, being fixed in submission to the Will of God. But one fear remained: he thought he might not be sufficiently brave at the final moment. However, the great and munificent goodness of God conquered that fear and overwhelmed it by stirring up in him so great an attachment to God and so fervent a loving desire to see Him that Niccolò lost his fear. He said, 'Stay with me; do not go away: when you are near, I cannot but be good, and I shall die happy.' He rested his head on my breast. Then did I understand the joy and the sweetness that stirred within his heart, and I knew as well that I myself wished to shed all my blood for the sweetest of spouses, Jesus.

"As I felt this desire well up in my heart, I thought of Niccolò's fear of not dying bravely, and I said to him: 'Have courage, dear brother, for now we go to the wedding feast. You will go cleansed in the sweet blood of God's Son; and I beg that you will not, even for an instant, be unmindful of the sweet name of Jesus. I will be with you on the scaffold!

"It was then that all fear left him and his sad countenance became joyful. Full of happiness, he said to me, in an exultant voice: 'How is it that so great a grace is given to me as to have the sweetness of my beloved go with me even to the holy place of justice?' As you see, he had attained to so high a degree of illumination, that he was able to speak of the place of execution as *holy*. Then he said: 'I go forth strong and glorious; but it seems to me that many years must pass before I meet you again here below or you come to me.' He spoke of the goodness of God in words of such sweetness that they could not fail to burn within the hearer's heart.

"Then I went to await Him at the place of execution. I stood by, and I prayed without ceasing, to Mary and to the virgin martyr Catherine. Before the arrival of Niccolò, I bent down and placed my own head upon the block.

"I had time before he came to recollect myself, and I raised my soul on high as best I could. I prayed, and I besought Our Lady, saying *Maria;* for I hoped that he might be given grace at the fatal moment, and be so filled with a sense of God's presence and with peace of heart that he would know he was going back to his Creator. The promise I had made was so deeply fixed in my heart that in the midst of that vast crowd I was simply incapable of recognizing anyone.

"Finally, he came forth, meek as a lamb. As soon as he saw me he began to smile. He had wished that I make the sign of the Cross over him. When I had made that holy sign I said: 'Bow your head, my dear brother; this is the wedding feast, and soon will you lay hold on everlasting life!' He bent forward with great gentleness, and I laid his head upon the block, bending over him and reminding him of the redeeming blood of the Lamb. He murmured ceaselessly: 'Jesus-Catherine.' And while he was yet saying these two names, I took his head into my hands.

"Then it was, that thinking fixedly of the divine goodness, I said: 'I will.' " [7]

To Christians of our own epoch, all the details of these events are extraordinary. The most remarkable thing about the whole affair is that it could have happened at all. Yet, it does not appear that contemporaries were shocked to see this young girl going into the dungeon of this twenty-year-old youth, nor to behold her standing on the scaffold the next day receiving his head in her hands. We are aware that Catherine of Siena has been canonized, and we are inclined, therefore, to see all that she did as good; but the boldness of her behavior will be apparent if, in imagination, we attribute it to some young girl in the congregation of some small parish of our own day. Decidedly, the Middle Ages possessed a frankness of manner, an uprightness of heart, and a health of soul which had been entirely lost by the time of St. Alphonsus de'Liguori; and we ourselves are far from having regained these qualities. It is not that there has been any abatement of grace, nor that revealed truth is more veiled from our eyes. The fact is that the temperament of Christians has grown insipid.

In offering for consideration the contrast which these two scenes present, I wish merely to ask the reader to avoid confusing holiness with some concrete and particular attitude; this can differ in one saint and in another according to their differences of temperament. I would like to say, too, that the deeds of the saints do not relieve the Christian of his own

[7] From the version of L. P. Guigues, after St. Catherine's original narration.

sense of judgment nor of his obligation to employ it. Each one of us is to seek, in the immensely varied chronicles of holiness, for the situations and the responses to them which are best accommodated to his own personal calling. In a decadent age like our own, when we suffer so much because of a lack of physical and moral strength, it is to be desired that young people should have set up as exemplars of holiness, saints who have been *doers of deeds* rather than *seekers for the reason of things,* hardy saints who, once they have become aware of God's will, have hastened to its most speedy accomplishment.

It is easy to see that a monk ought to be especially devoted to the imitation of the founder and of the other saints of his own order, as well as to the understanding of the doctors and mystics of that order. A soldier will be more drawn to saints who were themselves soldiers; while mothers of families will feel a strong attraction to St. Monica and to St. Elisabeth of Hungary. Recourse ought to be had to saints most likely to understand our own way of life, precisely because they have lived lives like ours. We should ponder upon the actual background of the lessons which the saints teach us, and the manner in which these lessons were taught by them, and we must give due consideration to the defects and virtues of the people to whom they actually spoke. For example—and it is something to be thought about carefully—a saint like John of the Cross had in mind, when he wrote, cloistered nuns; and, moreover, they were cloistered nuns in sixteenth-century Spain.

★　★　★

A Christian country is one that bends every effort
to be holy in the same degree that it strives to be a
fatherland. It is a country which, through its institutions and customs, expresses the spirit of Christ. It is
a country which finds the sources of its laws and public acts in the Gospel. These are truths which nowa-
days have so ceased to be a part of our consciousness
that to express them artlessly would be to court ridi-
cule. And yet Christ is King of nations as well as of
souls. Christ is the King; He is a king who reigns and
who ought to rule. Throughout the ages, how many
thousands of Frenchmen have there been who have
hoped in and lived for that supernatural right of rulership, how many have there been who have died for
the sake of His transcendent sovereignty! France of
the *ancien régime* found her deepest inner strength
in the *mystique* of a temporal Christendom.

I think there can be no question here of ambiva-
lence. I speak now of Christendom and of the role
of a country in the world's destiny. I am not speaking
here of the Church or of eternal life. To a Catholic it
is crystal clear that the Church is deathless, and that
she will accomplish the mission entrusted to her
alone, that is to say, that she will preserve intact the
content of Revelation, along with the actualities of
the sacramental life. But this mission can be dis-
charged even when the Church does not cover a very
extensive area or count among her flock a numerically
large group of faithful souls. The task was accomplished to perfection when the Church was shrouded
by the darkness of the catacombs; and, from the point
of view of her *nature,* it is of slight import that the
Church be visibly organized as a vast and powerful

corporation. Like a great pyramid set upon its apex, the Church is able to influence the world even if it touch it at only one narrow point.

It is otherwise with Christendom. Christendom represents the expression of an effort to build up and to organize temporal life in accordance with the principles of the Gospel. In this connection these principles are considered not alone as the kernels of divine and supernatural life, containing within themselves the germinating force for the salvation of souls, but mainly as the principles which underlie the construction of the earthly city, as master political concepts, as the means for achieving the present betterment of humankind, in accordance with the necessities of earthly survival and with due regard to the practical questions which concern mortal life, whether it be of the individual or of the community.

This renewal and upbuilding of the temporal Christendom is not committed to priestly pastors as such; for Christendom need not be a clerical theocracy: the temporal kingdom of God is rather in the hands of all men of good will, insofar as they must fulfil the mission in time which is given them. That it be more than a dream or a plan on paper, like Plato's *Republic,* the actualization of a Christendom requires a real social order, thoroughly impregnated by Christian principles but based upon earthly foundations. Christendom cannot flourish in the catacombs: it lives only under the open sky, and is in need of fresh air and space in which to grow; it must be made up of countless real men and women, of flesh and bone and muscle as well, who are thoroughly grounded in the spirit of the Gospel and resolved that, at whatever cost, not merely their personal conduct but the affairs which they regulate and the destiny of their country will also conform to that same spirit. This may seem like vain imagining; but it is, nevertheless, something which has had real existence and is no fantasy. Never did France show itself so true and so noble as under St. Louis. Never was there achieved a better blending of heroism and of courtesy.

The Gospel is ever open to our need of it, and is like the seed which waits to be sown in the earth. We shall see the rise of a new Christendom when young Christians have learned how to long for it. After all, it is but forty years ago that certain political doctrines which today are sown deeply in the lives of men and women were known only to little groups of initiates and enthusiasts who seemed mere utopians. It is true, of course, that the world is always ready to yield in the face of force. Therefore, it becomes the duty of Christians to see to it that justice be strong, lest it too be conquered by it. For force, after all, is like an amphibious animal: it functions equally well on seas of evil as on land which is good. Why should it be left to the cynical alone to harness this mastodon? Did not the spirit of force yield, aforetime, also to Francis of Assisi when he was heard to say: "My brother Wolf, in the name of God, I restrain you. . . ." And so will it again yield when young Christians courageously resist being gently thrust into the catacombs of social inactivity. Christendom has need of space and air. It is like a pyramid which is rightly set upon a broad human foundation, and of which the apex reaches up to the heaven of the Gospel revelation.

In the absence of such a foundation the social order cannot endure. It is for this reason that when a Christian civilization lacks a body it perishes. We are far from realizing the true repercussions of the real political revolution which the jurisconsults of the sixteenth century prepared by re-introducing Roman law, a revolution which has fulfilled itself during the entire modern age by exerting a natural opposition to the true spirit of Christianity. I should like to make reference here to a document which, ironically enough, is dated 1791. It is an ordinary maritime insurance policy, and it begins in these terms: "In the name of God and of the Blessed Virgin. May God guide all to salvation." And the conclusion is as follows: ". . . Then the said risk shall be ended. And it is agreed that all who are covered by the present insurance and have undergone similar peril, whether divine or human in origin, whether from friend or from enemy, known or unknown, whether of capture and imprisonment by either spiritual or temporal authority, of reprisals justified or not, of band or contraband, of marque or countermarque, of wind, storm, fire, of shipwreck, or of any other trouble, peril, or unforeseen happening which may come about, they having returned to their own ports and no breach of contract having been proven, payment shall be made three months after the authenticated news of the shipwreck or loss, which may God forfend; or recourse may afterwards be had to the courts for legal redress, should this seem desirable. . . . May God guide and save all. *Amen.*"

I do not contend that either Sieur Nicolas or Sieur Bourguignon, who signed this document, were saints. I merely state that this simple juridical formulary of the insurance contract demonstrates the existence of a real sense of Divine Providence, of God's care of us and of His almighty nearness to us in all the spiritual and temporal occurrences of our lives. It did not seem to them unfitting to God's majesty or to the holiness of Our Lady that they watch over the cargo carried upon a brigantine. And the reality of these two presences so colored the minds and thoughts of Christian people that notaries and policemen—to say nothing of others—considered those presences in respect to the soundness of a contract in which Christians joined. The worth of these contracts, their binding force and real validity, was worth exactly as much as the Christian fidelity of those who signed them. Yet it was the practice itself which, in its actual expression, served as the embodiment of this fidelity. Their juridical expression being thus humanly assured, these practices were directed toward God: it is because of this and of the fact that they were in accord with true Christian consciences that they themselves acquired that real purity and that vital strength which flow from sanctity, from having being directed toward God.

This holiness was expressed in the public institutions of the past and in its customs, being of great help to the poorest of wretches—whom it made Christians almost without their being aware of it— but it has almost disappeared from the world of our own day. The harvests of past years cannot be relied on indefinitely, and our own generation has found that the granaries are empty. What little of the ancient spirit we now hold on to will not suffice for ourselves and for those who will follow us. At the point to which we, are come we are obliged to sow new seed in order to have the hope of not dying of hunger. On this point restrictions are no longer enough; it has been so long since the Christian spirit has functioned in government. I am quite aware that in this laicized world of ours we have nevertheless had St. Thérèse of the Child Jesus and all those Carmels whence sanctity flows, after its price has been paid. But I am now concerned rather with the question of the whole order of Christian civilization, and from this point of view one may well compare personal holiness to a sort of mystical black market of very limited extent. What is really needed is a means of affording nourishment to all those poor wretches who are unable to make the great act of renunciation of self, but who wish, nevertheless, while they are living decently and doing their best by ordinary standards in the workaday world, to save their souls besides.

It is of these unfortunates that I am thinking, of the people who are outlandishly termed "the mass of the thrifty." In the spiritual as well as in the financial order, the great depressions bring heaviest suffering to the countless numbers of unknowns who are, in spite of appearances, the great *reserve* of a people or of a race. Christendom is a society wherein Christ lives with the poor and helps them in their day-to-day travail.

The same psychological deviation within the heart of the Christian religion which has produced the devotee has its equivalent, socially, in the type of state where religion is officially established but which remains nevertheless un-Christian. This type of state conceives of religion as being primarily an external assurance, a divine consecration of the established order. Like the devotee, it lives under the shadow of fear. It fears extinction, as the devotee fears hell. Now actually it is not by fear of them that either the revolution or hell is best avoided: all that is necessary is to seek first the kingdom of God and His justice—and as for the rest, let the will of God be done. The saint knows that God loves His children. Christendom feels the same assurance; it is able, therefore, to go forward in obedience to the evangelical spirit. All the heroism of Christendom is the fruit of the hope which is grounded in the spirit of the Gospel. Nevertheless, as we well know, there can be no Christian social order which lacks its experience of the Cross. Christian societies cannot escape suffering: it is, in fact, the very law of their temporal health and of their greatness.

A Christian state, then, is by no means a society which is directed politically by the foolishly devout, and which shares their spirit. Most assuredly, too, the state in which religion is merely officially established is no more an embodiment of Christendom than is the devotee an embodiment of the Church: one as much as the other, lacking as they both are in generosity of spirit, is athirst for the love of others. Christendom is a state which belongs to Christ, an earthly country where Christ is at home.

Let us carefully recall the conditions which govern and regulate human sanctity, that respect for nature which grace penetrates without extinguishing it. *Non minuit sed sacravit.* No society ever becomes Christian by the loss of its real nature or of its human qualities. Contrariwise, it is in this growth and realization that human liberty most fully exercises its own rôle, for there can be no holiness without liberty, just because there can be no holiness without love. Christendom is a society perfect and at unity within itself because in its laws, in its institutions, and in its customs it directs itself with resolute freedom and all loyalty to Christ.

It appears to me that all that has been said by St. Thomas Aquinas in respect to the common good requiring political action cannot be considered apart from the entire understanding of that part of the *Summa* which deals with morality, a morality deriving its force only in the light of the Christology of Aquinas, for he has shown that all moral laws and principles converge in the Adorable Person of the crucified Saviour. There can, indeed, be no common good of Christendom unless it be centered in Christ and in His holy will. Herod, "that fox," was not of Christ. Neither can mere political realism be sufficient for the common good of Christendom. St. Louis was no fox; but, on the other hand, many great political leaders have betrayed—to the degree that they have shown themselves to be foxes—that quality of belonging to Christ which is the vital bond of Christianity. If we are to remake of our country a Christian state, we must break with all that compromises purity and moral strength; for it is these that are the characteristics vitally essential to a nation centered in God in the order of its practical policies.

"There is no need that even one among us—doing our duty to profession, our country, work, or family, our poor faces etched in agony, our hands hardened by toil, beset by the wearisome round of daily life as we strive to earn our bread and keep our homes— there is no need that one of us ever know enough theology to become a canon. Yet we do know enough to become saints. We may leave it to others peaceably to govern the kingdom of God! We have all we can do to live hour by hour, passing in the midst of our difficulties from one to another of the hours of a day which seems endless, until there shall come that long- awaited hour, that special hour, in which God will deign to breathe upon His exhausted child. O death full of refreshment! O only dawn! Let others look after spiritual affairs. . . . It is to temporal concerns that we have set our hands, and those hands are fully employed in the affairs of God's temporal kingdom. We are the inheritors of the saints: with us are blessed the vines and the sheaves, the stones of our door- steps, the roofs whereon the doves are nesting, our poor cots given over to dreams and forgetfulness, the roads over which trucks are grinding by, our smiling sons and our daughters who sob beside the waterfalls; and it is God himself who has visited us. Is there any- thing in this world which our saints ought not recap- ture? Is there anything which they are not able to give?" [8]

[8] Bernanos, *Jeanne relapse et sainte,* pp. 67-8.